T0328687

Cambridge Elements ≡

Elements in Organization Theory
edited by
Nelson Phillips
UC Santa Barbara
Royston Greenwood
University of Alberta

AMBIGUITY IN ORGANIZATION THEORY

From Intrinsic to Strategic Perspectives

Giulia Cappellaro
Bocconi University

Amelia Compagni
Bocconi University

Eero Vaara
University of Oxford

CAMBRIDGE
UNIVERSITY PRESS

CAMBRIDGE
UNIVERSITY PRESS

Shaftesbury Road, Cambridge CB2 8EA, United Kingdom

One Liberty Plaza, 20th Floor, New York, NY 10006, USA

477 Williamstown Road, Port Melbourne, VIC 3207, Australia

314–321, 3rd Floor, Plot 3, Splendor Forum, Jasola District Centre, New Delhi – 110025, India

103 Penang Road, #05–06/07, Visioncrest Commercial, Singapore 238467

Cambridge University Press is part of Cambridge University Press & Assessment, a department of the University of Cambridge.

We share the University's mission to contribute to society through the pursuit of education, learning and research at the highest international levels of excellence.

www.cambridge.org
Information on this title: www.cambridge.org/9781009358439

DOI: 10.1017/9781009358460

First published 2023

A catalogue record for this publication is available from the British Library.

ISBN 978-1-009-35843-9 Paperback
ISSN 2397-947X (online)
ISSN 2514-3859 (print)

Ambiguity in Organization Theory

From Intrinsic to Strategic Perspectives

Elements in Organization Theory

DOI: 10.1017/9781009358460
First published online: January 2023

Giulia Cappellaro
Bocconi University

Amelia Compagni
Bocconi University

Eero Vaara
University of Oxford

Author for correspondence: Giulia Cappellaro, giulia.cappellaro@unibocconi.it

Abstract: This Element presents and discusses the main trajectories in the evolution of the concept of ambiguity and the most relevant theoretical contributions developed around it. It specifically elaborates on both the intrinsic perspectives on ambiguity as an inherent part of organizational decision-making processes and the more recent strategic perspectives on discursively constructed strategic ambiguity. It helps illuminate the path ahead of organizational scholars and offers new avenues for future research. This is important given the ever more pervasive presence of ambiguity in and around organizations and societies.

This Element also has a video abstract: www.cambridge.org/Organization Theory_Giulia Cappellaro_abstract

Keywords: ambiguity, decision-making, strategy, organizational discourse and communication, organizational change

ISBNs: 9781009358439 (PB), 9781009358460 (OC)
ISSNs: 2397-947X (online), 2514-3859 (print)

Contents

Worlds in which interpretation and desires are contradictory
and causality is unfathomable can be disturbing. They are represented
in fairy tales by the forest (dark, forbidding, and dangerous) and
in stories of adventure by the sea (dark, powerful, and uncontrollable).
Ambiguous worlds are disturbing, but they are also magical.
Beauty and ugliness are compounded; reality and fantasy are intertwined;
history is created; intelligence is expanded.
(March, Primer on decision making: How decisions happen, 1994: 179)

1 Introduction

The purpose of this Element is to focus on the concept of ambiguity and explain what it means as an inherent part of organization theory. Ambiguity can be broadly defined as a lack of clarity regarding a phenomenon or situation (Feldman, 1991; Weick, 1995) or the presence of multiple, even conflicting, interpretations of the same phenomenon (Daft & Weick, 1984; Feldman, 1989). In this Element, we argue that ambiguity is a key feature of organizational and social phenomena and that it deserves special attention because it helps us understand fundamental aspects of the social construction of the reality around us. Focusing on ambiguity offers a fruitful perspective for understanding the multiplicity of goals, interests, values, perspectives, and voices that characterize contemporary organizations – and how they may or may not coexist. By so doing, it helps us to move from the conventional views of organizations as monolithic entities with clear features and objectives to an understanding that highlights the fuzziness, unpredictability, and irrationality of organizational decision-making and organizational life more generally.

It is no wonder that ambiguity has played a role in organization theory for a long time – almost from the start. This is especially the case with the seminal work of James March (Cohen, March, & Olsen, 1972; Cyert & March, 1963; March, 2010), which has highlighted the key role of ambiguity in organizational decision-making. For quite some time, scholars have also been interested in how organizations cope with various circumstances of environmental ambiguity or uncertainty (Tushman & Nadler, 1978; Tushman & O'Reilly, 1996). A specific stream of research has developed around causal ambiguity (Konlechner & Ambrosini, 2019), highlighting the difficulties inherent in understanding the antecedents or consequences of organizational decisions or actions. More recently, we have seen an important shift from a more limited focus on decision-making to a view of ambiguity as a key part of the social construction of reality. In particular, rooted in communication studies (Eisenberg, 1984), we have seen an increasing interest in strategic ambiguity and how it may be deliberately used by organizational actors. One can also see connections with discursive, poststructuralist, and postmodern analysis of the multiple realities in and around organizations (Phillips & Oswick, 2012).

What is important for our purposes is the significant broadening that has occurred in our understanding of ambiguity. Although it is widely established that ambiguity can create major problems in organizations (Alvesson & Sveningsson, 2003; Denis, Langley, & Cazale, 1996), the more recent studies have shown how it can also help mobilize people for common causes (Sillince, Jarzabkowski, & Shaw, 2012) and provide strategic advantages in a variety of contexts (Cappellaro, Compagni, & Vaara, 2021; Eisenberg, 1984). It is this more recently "discovered" strategic perspective on ambiguity that deserves special attention and is a particular reason for this Element.

Over time, the concept of ambiguity has been progressively disentangled from related terms such as uncertainty (Townsend et al., 2018), paradox (Fairhurst et al., 2016), multivocality (Padgett & Ansell, 1993), and polyphony (Belova, King, & Sliwa, 2008). However, despite long-standing interest in ambiguity in organization theory, we lack integrative and systematic analyses of the various types, dimensions, and uses of *ambiguity in and around organizations*. This has hampered fruitful exchange between scholars from different traditions and impeded the overall theoretical development of this crucial aspect of organization theory. We believe that conceptually integrated research and critical reflection on organizational ambiguity are particularly relevant for theoretical discussion of strategic decisions in organizations in the fluid and often unpredictable context that characterizes our current social reality.

In this Element, we offer such a framework. We will start with a discussion of adjacent and partly overlapping research on related concepts. This will lead us to a review of what we label intrinsic and early perspectives on ambiguity in organization studies as they relate to goals, causes, context, information, and categories and focus on organizational decision-making processes. We will then proceed to an overview of more recent perspectives focusing on strategic ambiguity. This will lead us to present a path forward in research on ambiguity in organization theory and an agenda for future research. In all this, we attempt to take a broad and comprehensive perspective; we seek to situate ideas about ambiguity in their intellectual context and then explain what they mean for here and now in our integrative approach. While this means some key linkages to research in other areas – such as political science or communication studies – we will focus on organizational ambiguity and primarily deal with how it shapes decisions and actions in and around organizations.

2 Ambiguity versus Other Concepts

Over time, a number of constructs and terms have been associated or used interchangeably with ambiguity – especially uncertainty, paradox, equivocality, or polyphony – making sometimes difficult a clear definition of this construct. What do these different streams of work imply for ambiguity? One alternative is to see them as separate but overlapping trajectories of work and seek to define ambiguity as something distinctively different. The other alternative is to acknowledge and build on the overlaps to offer a more comprehensive – and thus holistic – view of ambiguity as a central organizational concept and multifaceted phenomenon. This is the approach we take in this Element. We view ambiguity as a fundamental concept and phenomenon that can also help clarify certain aspects of other constructs. Specifically, we see uncertainty as a precursor of ambiguity, equivocality as a key type of ambiguity, paradox as constitutive of contradictory viewpoints and therefore of ambiguity, and finally polyphony as a manifestation of ambiguity in discourses or narratives. In this section we briefly review each of these constructs and elaborate on the relationship with ambiguity.

2.1 Uncertainty

Uncertainty is a term that has been used more frequently than ambiguity in various disciplines and streams of research. In fact, uncertainty is a key component in studies of decision-making because it denotes a typical condition in organizational reality: unknowingness. More specifically, scholars in cognitive psychology, decision sciences, and – most importantly for us – organization studies have focused on how to deal with uncertainty and its implications (Cyert & March, 1963; March & Simon, 1958; Tversky & Kahneman, 1974; Williamson, 1979). During the 1960s, Burns and Stalker (1961) studied how different organizational forms were able to innovate based on their ability to cope with environmental uncertainty. Later, scholars have looked at how and whether organizations could cope with the need for organizational change in order to respond to pressures from uncertain or ambiguous environments (e.g., Tushman & Nadler, 1978; Tushman & O'Reilly, 1996).

Such uncertainty has usually been seen as the inability to foresee the consequences of specific decision or action alternatives. Thus, the focus in this body of work has been forward-looking, that is, it has dealt with the uncertainty of specific choices regarding future outcomes. Oftentimes this body of work has included a normative undertone in that uncertainty has been seen as a problem or challenge for individuals and organizations. Moreover, much of the research has aimed at offering models for dealing with uncertainty and essentially making more informed or otherwise better decisions.

Despite the fact that uncertainty and ambiguity have been often paired in the literature, distinctions have been made. Attempts to disentangle uncertainty from ambiguity have come, for instance, from research on entrepreneurship that has often focused on the uncertainty faced by new entrepreneurs and ventures (Packard, Clark, & Klein, 2017; Townsend et al., 2018). For instance, Townsend et al. (2018) have called for a distinction between uncertainty as a special kind of knowledge problem involving probabilistic reasoning about the consequences of specific actions and other types of knowledge problems such as ambiguity complexity, and equivocality. An important distinction between uncertainty and ambiguity is also made by March (1994) and Weick (1995). They explain, in somewhat different ways, how uncertainty is closely connected to a lack of information and, as such, can be partially overcome by collecting more facts. Ambiguity, instead, is associated with lack of clarity in meaning or with a confusing plurality of meaning, and, as such, can be partially solved only by acquiring or creating interpretative frames or "explanatory knowledge" (Zack, 2000). In this way, uncertainty can be seen as a precursor of ambiguity.

2.2 Equivocality

Equivocality is a term used especially in sensemaking research (Weick, 1995) to denote a situation of confusion, in which multiple, conflicting interpretations seem all plausible. In this sense, equivocality can be considered a key type of ambiguity, and it is not surprising, therefore, that the two terms have been frequently used interchangeably in the literature (Daft & Macintosh, 1981). As Weick suggests, in an equivocal situation, "people are not sure what questions to ask, nor do they expect clear answers even if they do know the right questions" (1995: 9). In sensemaking studies, equivocality plays a key role (Maitlis & Christianson, 2014; Navis & Glynn, 2011). First, equivocality appears to permeate organizational reality. This is because "events occur in a continuously emerging context that changes the meaning of earlier events, and partly because events occur in an open-ended retrospective context in which all kinds of prior personal and societal history can be invoked to explain what is happening" (Weick, 1995: 10). Second, interpreting events and giving it a meaning in the absence of "fixed unequivocal observables" can only lead, according to Weick, to a "network of interdependent and continuously modifiable interpretations" (Weick, 1995: 10). This may in turn engender confusion in and around organizations that needs to be made sense of. In other words, as Weick (1979) suggests, the only viable response to equivocality is equivocality itself. Sensemaking is, indeed, the attempt to come to some sort of temporary consensus around how to interpret events and what to make of them. Under conditions of equivocality, "efforts are made to construct a plausible sense of what is happening, and this sense of plausibility normalizes the breach, restores the expectation, and enables projects to continue" (Weick, Sutcliffe, & Obstfeld, 2005: 414–415).

In many classic studies of sensemaking, equivocality has most often been regarded as a problem for sensemaking. The multiple interpretations and especially misinterpretations originating in equivocal situations have been seen as the causes of accidents, crises, or disasters (Cornelissen, Mantere, & Vaara, 2014; Weick, 1993; Weick & Sutcliffe, 2001; Weick, Sutcliffe, & Obstfeld, 2005). In some of these instances, equivocality is linked with collapse in sensemaking (Weick, 1993, 1995). For example, Weick's classic study of the Mann Gulch disaster illustrates how people may experience a "cosmology" episode void of meaning, implying a lack of understanding of what is important, what to focus on, why, and how. These special situations involve more than equivocality – in fact all kinds of ambiguity. Nevertheless, it may be equivocality – and the different interpretations made of the disaster – that has specific implications for the outcomes of decisions and actions.

Overall, we believe that in organization studies equivocality is the construct closest to ambiguity – as defined in the introduction to this Element – and we propose to consider it as a type or instance of ambiguity linked specifically to possibility of interpreting situations or cues in multiple ways.

2.3 Paradox

In treating ambiguity, it is important to pay special attention to the construct of paradox – especially as there has recently been a surge of research employing this concept (Putnam, Fairhurst, & Banghart, 2016; Schad et al., 2016; Smith & Lewis, 2011). Studies on paradox have mainly explored situations characterized by tensions, contradictions, dualisms, and dialectics in and around organizations. This has essentially meant broadening the traditional view in philosophy that construes paradox as a logically untenable or incomprehensible situation created by two or more opposite or contradictory facts or characteristics (Sorensen, 2003). This research has increasingly placed paradox and related phenomena in discourses, social interaction processes, practices, and ongoing organizational activities rather than in cognition (Luscher, Lewis, & Ingram, 2006; Putnam, Fairhurst, & Banghart, 2016).

In one of the first reviews on paradox (Lewis, 2000) in organization theory, Lewis defines paradox as a situation denoting "contradictory yet interrelated elements – elements that seem logical in isolation but absurd and irrational when appearing simultaneously" (2000: 760). Later on, Putnam, Fairhurst, and Banghart (2016) extend this definition and elaborate how tension (stress, anxiety, discomfort, tightness in making choices or moving forward in organizational situations), dualisms (opposite poles, dichotomies, binary relationships), dualities (inter-dependence of opposites in a relationship that is not mutually exclusive or antagonistic), contradictions (bipolar opposites that are mutually exclusive and interdependent so that opposites define and potentially negate each other), and dialectics (interdependent opposites aligned with forces that exert push-pull on each other in ongoing dynamic interplay) represent all paradoxical situations in organizations (Farjoun, 2016).

Ambiguity has been often associated with paradox (Cappellaro, Compagni, & Vaara, 2021; Hatch & Erhlich, 1993; Luscher, Lewis, & Ingram, 2006), although their relationship has been rarely discussed in an explicit way. For instance, Putnam (1986) indicates how contradictory messages might engender ambiguity in organizational actors as in lack of clarity about what action to take. Others have talked about a sense of confusion and paralysis (Luscher, Lewis, & Ingram, 2006) in response to a paradoxical situation. Hatch and Erhlich (1993) draw a further connection between paradox and ambiguity. In their paper, they describe how using a decision-making frame to face a paradoxical issue might indeed bring actors to perceive ambiguity:

> This ambiguity may result from the use of a rational decision-making frame of reference for handling a situation characterized by incongruity, contradiction and incoherence. In rational decision-making processes, problems are assumed to have solutions and the two categories (problem and solution) are assumed distinguishable. In the case at hand, problems and solutions are not clear-cut categories because the underlying paradox of control keeps creating unintended consequences for the choices made. These unintended consequences transform solutions into problems. Thus, we suggest that the continued application of a rational decision-making frame to a paradoxical issue may produce ambiguity for decision-makers. (1993: 519–520)

In most of these instances, the construct of paradox appears to be distinguishable from ambiguity and to work as one of its antecedent.

2.4 Polyphony

Polyphony is another construct related to ambiguity. In the literature, polyphony is also referred to as polyvocality, plurivocality, multivocality, or even heteroglossia. Although it refers to a multiplicity of voices, in essence the voices do not have to be contradictory as in paradox; they can instead be complementary or simply representations of different realities, identities, or perspectives (Letiche, 2010). The roots of polyphony can be found in Bakhtin's work on literary theory (Bakhtin, 1982), and it has thereafter become a very useful lens, especially in narrative or discourse analysis in organization studies (Belova, King, & Sliwa, 2008; Boje, 2008; Hazen, 1993).

This perspective does not necessarily imply a critical approach to organizations but is often used for critical analysis of the selective marginalization of voices or silencing in organizations.

In this view, polyphony characterizes organizations and many organizational processes, and thus dialogicality is seen as a fundamental part of organizational sensemaking. Although multiple voices can be seen as problematic (Sullivan & McCarthy, 2008) for organizations, most often polyphony is valued; for instance, Bakhtinian analysis sees "carnival" as the fullest and, in this sense, the ideal type of polyphony (Bakhtin, 1984) that can develop within organizations. In this respect, polyphony – as expressed in the plurality of voices and narratives present at any time in organizations – and ambiguity are both fundamental and natural parts of organizational life. In a nutshell, polyphony can be seen as a manifestation of ambiguity in discourses or narratives.

3 Analytical Approach

To achieve the purpose of the Element – that is, develop a conceptually integrated framework and critical reflection on organizational ambiguity – we followed a three-step approach. First, we started by reading the seminal work on ambiguity in organization theory and we subsequently traced how the concept has evolved, performing an analysis of the empirical and conceptual studies published between 1950 and 2021. The analysis was based on two major databases (*Business Source Complete* and *Web of Science*). In both databases, we used the term(s) ambigu* in the title, abstract, or subject terms for the period between 1950 and 2021. We retrieved articles, books, and book chapters while excluding commentaries, letters, and book reviews. We then selected articles based on their publication outlet. We used a combination of three sets of journals: (i) the *Financial Times* top journals in management and marketing;[1] (ii) 4 or 4* outlets in the management, marketing, psychology, or sociology categories according to the UK Association of Business Schools;[2] and (iii) an additional selection of journal outlets in political science and public administration.[3]

---

[1] *Academy of Management Journal, Academy of Management Review, Accounting, Organizations and Society, Human Relations, Journal of Applied Psychology, Journal of Business Ethics, Journal of Consumer Research, Journal of International Business Studies, Journal of Management Studies, Journal of Marketing, Management Science, MIS Quarterly, Organization Science, Organization Studies, Organizational Behavior and Human Decision Processes, Research Policy, Strategic Management Journal.*

[2] We focused on categories labeled: psychology general and organizational; sociology; marketing; management both general management/ethics/gender/social responsibility and human resource management/employment studies; innovation management; operations research and management science; organization studies; strategy.

[3] *American Political Science Review, American Journal of Political Science, Journal of Public Administration Research and Theory Public Administration, Public Administration Review.*

This resulted in a set of 2,903 publications. By reading the abstracts, we categorized publications on the basis of their relevance and excluded those in which the analysis of ambiguity was not central to the publication, thereby obtaining a total of 698 publications. We then adopted the following analytical process. First, we read the abstracts of all 698 publications focusing on the definition of ambiguity, the theoretical underpinnings of the study (e.g., sense-making, decision-making, and strategy) and the role attributed to ambiguity. Being interested in how ambiguity and organizational phenomena are related, we screened the 698 publications for those studies that explicitly referred to the organizational level of analysis. We thus excluded papers referring to (i) individual roles, as in many articles on role ambiguity; (ii) individual decision-making processes, as in many articles in psychology and marketing, and (iii) ambiguity operationalized as a variable in formal models of decision-making or operations research with no reference to the organizational level.

Second, based on this dataset, we inductively reconstructed the main analytical perspectives on organizational ambiguity (contextual ambiguity, information ambiguity, goal ambiguity, causal ambiguity, category ambiguity, frame ambiguity, rhetorical ambiguity, and narrative/discursive ambiguity). For more emergent streams of literature, which we considered particularly promising for their potential contribution to theory, we searched through the references lists of the retrieved studies for additional papers and books. Overall, our final dataset comprises 148 publications.

Third, this then served as a basis for our theorization and development of the integrative framework presented in the next section. In particular, we focused on two meta-conceptualizations of ambiguity: ambiguity as an intrinsic part of organizational decision-making (intrinsic perspectives) and discursively constructed strategic ambiguity (strategic perspectives). We then dug deeper into the specific types and processes characterizing these perspectives. Finally, this led us to focus on what is lacking in existing literature and to develop ideas for future research.

4 Intrinsic Perspectives: Ambiguity as an Inherent Part of Organizational Decision-Making

The purpose of this section is to offer an overview of intrinsic perspectives on ambiguity. What we label intrinsic views depict ambiguity as a key part of organizational decision-making processes and action more generally. This view builds upon the traditions of bounded rationality – based on Herbert Simon's seminal work in cognitive psychology (Simon, 1947) – and the behavioral theory of the firm – based on James March's work (Cyert & March, 1963; March, 1958).

4.1 Seminal Research on Ambiguity as an Intrinsic Part of Organizational Decision-Making: The Work of James March

The roots of the work on ambiguity in organization studies and theory can be traced back to the seminal work of James March. In particular, his work on the garbage can model (Cohen, March, & Olsen, 1972) and organized anarchies (Cohen & March, 1974; March & Olsen, 1976) has offered a way to conceptualize and approach ambiguity as an inherent part of organizational decision-making and organizations in general.

4.1.1 Ambiguity, Uncertainty, and Bounded Rationality

The treatment of ambiguity by James March originates from his close collaboration with Herbert Simon and their common interest in how individuals in organizations make decisions collectively. Already in their co-authored 1958 book titled *Organizations*, March and Simon link concepts of ambiguity and uncertainty with that of limited or bounded rationality (Simon, 1947) in processes of decision-making. In contrast to the pure rationality theorized by neoclassical economics, the concept of bounded rationality implies that organizations can proceed rationally but not necessarily intelligently:

> Organizations are rational in intent and in the ways they justify their choices (they are procedurally rational), but their pursuit of rationality does not assure either coherent or intelligent action (often their actions are not substantively rational) (March & Simon, 1958: 8).

More specifically, bounded rationality means that certain elements and steps in decision-making are not optimal, as portrayed by normative decision-making theories. In particular, March and Simon (1958) emphasize that "people [in organizations] are often misinformed, or lack information, or are unable to predict or even compute the consequences of their actions. Their goals may sometimes be well-specified and stable, but often are unclear, inconsistent, and changing" (1958: 8). Hence, the two authors characterize uncertainty and ambiguity as pervasive in organizations.

March (1978) subsequently spells out the two steps in decision-making frequently affected by uncertainty and ambiguity respectively. In doing so, he makes a distinction between the two terms. The first step is that of anticipating the future consequences of current actions; it is affected by people's limited capacity to understand cause–effect relationships and accurately predict the consequences of alternative actions. According to March, "theories of choice under uncertainty emphasize the complications of guessing future consequences" (1978: 589). In this view, organizations cannot be certain about whether actions will help them solve a problem or reach a goal. The second step in decision-making linked to ambiguity, which March calls "confusing," involves anticipation of future prefer-ences. Contrary to normative theories of decision-making, March proposes that preferences – alternatively labeled as tastes, valued outcomes, or goals – are vague, problematic, inconsistent, and unstable (Cohen & March, 1974; March & Olsen, 1976) and hence in making decisions individuals and organizations experience a sense of ambiguity about their true priority in taking the actions in question. In subsequent work, March often refers to goal ambiguity as a condition permeating most organizational decision-making processes and making organ-izations into organized anarchies (Cohen & March, 1974).

According to March, ambiguity of goals is experienced by each individual. In other words, individual preferences are often "fuzzy and inconsistent" and "change over time" (March, 1978: 589). At the same time, ambiguity of goals is also an organizational and collective experience based on the intrinsic pluralism of organizations, that is, the presence of multiple actors and con-flicting objectives that do nothing but amplify the ambiguity associated with individual goals. The conduciveness of the organizational context in feeding ambiguity is also manifest in the so-called garbage can model of decision-making proposed by Cohen, March, and Olsen (1972). In this model, not only do participants enter and exit the decision venue fluidly, but the extent of the attention they focus on the issue at stake also varies over time. This makes the combination of goals inconsistent and even temporally misaligned with the actions and solutions proposed at any time, thereby creating a situation of ambiguity that is intrinsic to the political nature of organizations (March, 1962; March & Simon, 1958). Given that organizations are constituted by different coalitions of actors (March, 1962, 1994) expressing different inter-ests and goals, and given the politics of organizational roles and dynamics (Cohen, March, & Olsen, 1972), it is not surprising that goals within a single organization may not only be multiple but also be conflicting and mutually inconsistent, thereby engendering a sense of "confusion" in those who make organizational decisions.

In his book *A Primer on Decision Making*, March appears to further broaden the conceptualization of ambiguity beyond the sole idea of ambiguous goals:

> Ambiguity refers to a lack of clarity or consistency in reality, causality, or intentionality. Ambiguous situations are situations that cannot be coded precisely into mutually exhaustive and exclusive categories. Ambiguous purposes are intentions that cannot be specified clearly. Ambiguous identities are identities whose rules or occasions for application are imprecise or contradictory. Ambiguous outcomes are outcomes whose characters or impli-cations are fuzzy. Ambiguous histories are histories that do not provide unique, comprehensible interpretations. (March, 1994: 178)

Here March points to the fact that ambiguity, independently of its locus (e.g., goals, identity, or outcomes), is bound to be pervasive in most decision arenas within organizations, essentially any time meaning is "obscure" and the act of decision-making comes closer to an interpretative exercise (Beckman, 2021) than a perfect calculus, or, as March explains, a "calculus that allows the simultaneous existence of opposites and causal inconsistencies" (1994: 179). Hence ambiguity can derive from interpretation of the external reality and so-called events, from holding contradictory beliefs about a phenomenon that can be both true and false, from attempts to define one's own and others' identity, to specify preferences and desires, or to build from experiences (March, 2010).

4.1.2 Ambiguity as Both Natural and Sought-After

For the most part, ambiguity in March's view is naturally linked with how human beings reason and with their bounded rationality, to the point that the ambiguity of goals, the starting point in his conceptualization of ambiguity, should not be seen as an error or a sign of inadequacy in organizational decision-making, but rather as the logical and natural background in which decision-making occurs within organizations (March, 1978; March & Olsen, 1976). As March puts it this way:

> "Goal ambiguity, like limited rationality, is not necessarily a fault in human choice to be corrected but often a form of intelligence to be refined by the technology of choice rather than ignored by it" (March, 1978: 598).

Despite a conceptualization of ambiguity rooted in the cognitive capabilities of individuals and groups, March does not neglect to point out that this is not the only explanation of why people have ambiguous goals. Indeed, he suggests that ambiguity is not only something of which individuals are fundamentally aware but also something chosen and sought-after. He writes: "Human beings [. . .] know that no matter how much they may be pressured both by their own prejudices for integration and by the demands of others, they will be left with contradictory and intermittent desires partially ordered but imperfectly reconciled. As a result, they engage in activities designed to manage preferences or game preferences" (March, 1978: 598).

Hence individuals embrace ambiguity by constructing preferences, treating them strategically, and confounding, avoiding, or suppressing them. This may help organizational members achieve some results more easily. For instance, March repeatedly stresses in his work that ambiguity of goals may facilitate coalition-building within organizations (March, 1994). In this sense, March anticipates subsequent work on the strategic role of ambiguity, where it is exploited knowingly to "muddle through" the complexity of organizational processes.

With respect to more recent perspectives on strategic ambiguity, March is less focused on the role played by language and discourse in actually allowing individuals and organizations to embrace ambiguity (Levinthal & Rerup, 2021). He states that decision-making is indeed about talk and action (March, 1994) and that "understanding decision making involves understanding the ways in which language carries, elaborates, and creates meaning" (1994: 211–212). He notes that language may help clarify meaning but also create new ones, make metaphorical leaps, and thereby create ambiguity and equivocality. Yet, his focus is far from exploring the details of how language or talk may create such ambiguity, something that will instead be developed later by the scholarship on strategic ambiguity as discursively constructed (Section 5).

4.2 Organizational Scholarship on Ambiguity as an Intrinsic Part of Organizational Decision-Making

Building on the work and legacy of March and colleagues, a rich and varied body of work has emerged around ambiguity as an intrinsic part of organizational decision-making. In what follows, we identify and elaborate on five distinctive types of ambiguity as part of organizational decision-making. They refer to different loci of ambiguity: context, information, goals, cause–effect relationships, and categories. In the following, we present our interpretation of this research moving from inputs to outputs and from an internally elaborated to an externally evaluated condition.

Contextual ambiguity is associated with conditions at the environmental level (e.g., market, institutional, or societal) that affect organizational processes; it typically manifests itself in ambiguous policies, market conditions, or extreme settings. Such ambiguity is also embedded in organizational structures or authority relationships, specifically for certain typologies of organizations such as public bureaucracies or knowledge-intensive firms. *Information ambiguity* and *goal ambiguity* refer instead to whether the inputs for (e.g., evidence) or the outputs (e.g., objectives or targets) of the decision-making process are perceived as ambiguous. Third, *causal ambiguity* focuses on cause–effect relations in deciding on a certain course of action such as imitating another organization or competing with it. Finally, *category ambiguity* typically sees categories as "ambiguity-alleviators" and therefore ambiguity as a negative perception developed by external audiences regarding the existence of multiple divergent views of the same category, for example, in organizational features, market relationships, or prototype characteristics.

In most of these studies, ambiguity appears to have a negative impact on decision-making, either delaying its timing or biasing its results, with cumbersome implications for the actions and coordination efforts of organizations. Recent work on causal ambiguity and category ambiguity has advanced a more social conceptualization of the construct, showing how ambiguity may be desirable for some types of audiences and therefore sought-after by organizations. We argue that this view constitutes the transition to the more strategic conceptualization of ambiguity as strategically constructed. Table 1 summarizes the key characteristics of these types of ambiguity and provides further reading listing a sample of references.

4.2.1 Contextual Ambiguity

Contextual ambiguity can be seen as one of the most basic and natural forms of ambiguity; it represents a lack of understanding about the organization's environment and its implications for decisions and actions. Contextual ambiguity generally refers to situations where actors have to make decisions based on inadequate information and where circumstances are changing and novel (Zuzul, 2019). According to Ruefli and Sarrazin (1981), ambiguous circumstances involve uneven qualities and quantities of information, vaguely perceived strategic goals, and a diffuse decision-making process where decisions are made both inside and outside the firm. Stone and Brush (1996) define ambiguous contexts as situations where multiple constituencies have influence and where firms lack direct control over resource flows. In turn, Noval and Hernandez (2019) view contextual ambiguity as weak contextual cues represented by ambiguous claims to a resource.

Work on contextual ambiguity appears to focus more on the effects of ambiguity on groups, organizations, and decision-making processes and less on describing the ambiguity and contexts themselves. The effects of ambiguous contexts are generally negative and pose challenges. Ambiguous contexts can make people turn away from formal network ties and move toward informal and semiformal networks (Srivastava, 2015); they can make people too careful and cautious in making decisions (Gavetti & Warglien, 2015; Hsieh, Ma, & Novoselov, 2018) and even lead them to take random decisions that they or their peers might not otherwise take if more clarity was available (Walder, 2006). However, Rindova, Ferrier, and Wiltbank (2010) and Donnelly (2011) have stressed how ambiguous contexts can give organizations and firms a competitive edge and force them to innovate, even though ambiguity can be stressful for employees. Similarly, Lingo and O'Mahony (2010) have pointed to the positive opportunities in terms of invention and improvisation offered by ambiguous situations. Scholars highlight the role of individuals in making sense of ambiguous contexts (Coopey, Keegan, & Emler, 1998; Meszaros, 1999) and especially the

Table 1 Organizational scholarship on ambiguity as intrinsic element of organizational decision-making, by type and year

Author	Year	Article title	Journal
		Contextual ambiguity	
		• Ambiguity associated with contextual situations and conditions more or less explicitly described	
		• Various analytical levels impacting organizational processes: organizational, market, societal, and institutional	
Ruefli & Sarrazin	1981	Strategic control of corporate development under ambiguous circumstances.	*Management Science*
Duhaime & Schwenk	1985	Conjectures on cognitive simplification in acquisition and divestment decision-making.	*Academy of Management Review*
Purcell & Gray	1986	Corporate personnel departments and the management of industrial relations: Two case studies in ambiguity.	*Journal of Management Studies*
Kydd	1989	Understanding the information content in MIS management tools.	*MIS Quarterly*
Garud & Van de Ven	1992	An empirical evaluation of the internal corporate venturing process.	*Strategic Management Journal*
Alvesson	1993	Organizations as rhetoric: Knowledge-intensive firms and the struggle with ambiguity.	*Journal of Management Studies*
Adler	1995	Interdepartmental interdependence and coordination: The case of the design/manufacturing interface.	*Organization Science*
Stone & Brush	1996	Planning in ambiguous contexts: The dilemma of meeting needs for commitment and demands for legitimacy.	*Strategic Management Journal*
Coopey, Keegan, & Emler	1998	Managers' innovations and the structuration of organizations.	*Journal of Management Studies*

Author	Year	Title	Journal
Meszaros	1999	Preventive choices: Organizations' heuristics, decision processes and catastrophic risks.	Journal of Management Studies
Alvesson	2001	Knowledge work: Ambiguity, image and identity.	Human Relations
King & Ranft	2001	Capturing knowledge and knowing through improvisation: What managers can learn from the thoracic surgery board certification process.	Journal of Management
Pescosolido	2002	Emergent leaders as managers of group emotion.	The Leadership Quarterly
Alvesson & Sveningsson	2003	Good visions, bad micro-management and ugly ambiguity: Contradictions of (non) leadership in a knowledge-intensive organization.	Organization Studies
Carson, Madhok, & Wu	2006	Uncertainty, opportunism, and governance: The effects of volatility and ambiguity on formal and relational contracting.	Academy of Management Journal
Haas	2006	Knowledge gathering, team capabilities, and project performance in challenging work environments.	Management Science
Walder	2006	Ambiguity and choice in political movements: The origins of Beijing Red Guard factionalism.	American Journal of Sociology
Forbes	2007	Reconsidering the strategic implications of decision comprehensiveness.	Academy of Management Review
Rindova, Ferrier, & Wiltbank	2010	Value from gestalt: How sequences of competitive actions create advantage for firms in nascent markets.	Strategic Management Journal
Lingo & O'Mahony	2010	Nexus work: Brokerage on creative projects.	Administrative Science Quarterly
Donnelly	2011	The ambiguities and tensions in creating and capturing value: Views from HRM consultants in a leading consultancy firm.	Human Resource Management

Table 1 (cont.)

Author	Year	Article title	Journal
Petkova et al.	2014	Reputation and decision-making under ambiguity: A study of US venture capital firms' investments in the emerging clean energy sector.	*Academy of Management Journal*
Gavetti & Warglien	2015	A model of collective interpretation.	*Organization Science*
Srivastava	2015	Intraorganizational network dynamics in times of ambiguity.	*Organization Science*
Bridwell-Mitchell	2016	Collaborative institutional agency: How peer learning in communities of practice enables and inhibits micro-institutional change.	*Organization Studies*
Hsieh, Ma, & Novoselov	2018	Accounting conservatism, business strategy, and ambiguity.	*Accounting, Organizations and Society*
Wolbers, Boersma, & Groenewegen	2018	Introducing a fragmentation perspective on coordination in crisis management.	*Organization Studies*
Augustine et al.	2019	Constructing a distant future: Imaginaries in geoengineering.	*Academy of Management Journal*
Noval & Hernandez	2019	The unwitting accomplice: How organizations enable motivated reasoning and self-serving behavior.	*Journal of Business Ethics*

Information ambiguity

- Ambiguity associated with the information, evidence, or knowledge basis in decision-making processes
- Normally portrayed as hampering comprehension during decision-making

Author	Year	Article title	Journal
Daft & Macintosh	1981	A tentative exploration into the amount and equivocality of information processing in organizational work units.	*Administrative Science Quarterly*
Faircloth & Ricchiute	1981	Ambiguity intolerance and financial reporting alternatives.	*Accounting, Organizations and Society*

Author	Year	Title	Journal
Klein	1982	Performance, evaluation and the NHS: A case study in conceptual perplexity and organizational complexity.	*Public Administration*
Daft & Lengel	1986	Organizational information requirements, media richness and structural design.	*Management Science*
Schwenk	1988	Effects of devil's advocacy on escalating commitment.	*Human Relations*
Moussavi & Evans	1993	Emergence of organizational attributions: The role of a shared cognitive schema.	*Journal of Management*
Pich, Loch, & Meyer	2002	On uncertainty, ambiguity, and complexity in project management.	*Management Science*
Sgourev	2013	How Paris gave rise to Cubism (and Picasso): Ambiguity and fragmentation in radical innovation.	*Organization Science*
Wu & Zhang	2014	Home or overseas? An analysis of sourcing strategies under competition.	*Management Science*

Causal ambiguity

- Ambiguity associated with the incapacity to fully understand cause–effect relationships
- Mainly seen as impeding imitation and effective strategy-making

Author	Year	Title	Journal
Reed & DeFillippi	1990	Causal ambiguity, barriers to imitation, and sustainable competitive advantage.	*Academy of Management Review*
Rajagopalan & Finkelstein	1992	Effects of strategic orientation and environmental change on senior management reward systems.	*Strategic Management Journal*

Table 1 (cont.)

Author	Year	Article title	Journal
Lei, Hitt, & Bettis	1996	Dynamic core competences through meta-learning and strategic context.	*Journal of Management*
Szulanski	1996	Exploring internal stickiness: Impediments to the transfer of best practice within the firm.	*Strategic Management Journal*
Mosakowski	1997	Strategy making under causal ambiguity: Conceptual issues and empirical evidence.	*Organization Science*
Coff	1999	When competitive advantage doesn't lead to performance: The resource-based view and stakeholder bargaining power.	*Organization Science*
McEvily, Das, & McCabe	2000	Avoiding competence substitution through knowledge sharing.	*Academy of Management Review*
King & Zeithaml	2001	Competencies and firm performance: Examining the causal ambiguity paradox.	*Strategic Management Journal*
Lockett & Thompson	2001	The resource-based view and economics.	*Journal of Management*
Szulanski, Cappetta, & Jensen	2004	When and how trustworthiness matters: Knowledge transfer and the moderating effect of causal ambiguity.	*Organization Science*
Powell, Lovallo, & Caringal	2006	Causal ambiguity, management perception, and firm performance.	*Academy of Management Review*
Gottschalg & Zollo	2007	Interest alignment and competitive advantage.	*Academy of Management Review*
King	2007	Disentangling interfirm and intrafirm causal ambiguity: A conceptual model of causal ambiguity and sustainable competitive advantage.	*Academy of Management Review*

Author	Year	Title	Journal
Cording, Christmann, & King	2008	Reducing causal ambiguity in acquisition integration: Intermediate goals as mediators of integration decisions and acquisition performance.	Academy of Management Journal
Inkpen	2008	Knowledge transfer and international joint ventures: The case of NUMMI and General Motors.	Strategic Management Journal
Ryall	2009	Causal ambiguity, complexity, and capability-based advantage.	Management Science
Ambrosini & Bowman	2010	The impact of causal ambiguity on competitive advantage and rent appropriation.	British Journal of Management
Boyd, Bergh, & Ketchen	2010	Reconsidering the reputation – performance relationship: A resource-based view.	Journal of Management
Lakshman	2011	Postacquisition cultural integration in mergers & acquisitions: A knowledge-based approach.	Human Resource Management
Szulanski, Ringov, & Jensen	2016	Overcoming stickiness: How the timing of knowledge transfer methods affects transfer difficulty.	Organization Science
Vermeulen	2018	A basic theory of inheritance: How bad practice prevails.	Strategic Management Journal
Feldman, Ozcan, & Reichstein	2019	Falling not far from the tree: Entrepreneurs and organizational heritage.	Organization Science
Konlechner & Ambrosini	2019	Issues and trends in causal ambiguity research: A review and assessment.	Journal of Management

Table 1 (cont.)

Author	Year	Article title	Journal
		Goal ambiguity	
		• Ambiguity associated with the incapacity to fully define goals, objectives, or targets	
		• Often referred to public managers and organizations operating in the public sector	
Turcotte	1974	Control systems, performance, and satisfaction in two state agencies.	*Administrative Science Quarterly*
Schramm	1975	Thompson's assessment of organizations: Universities and the AAUP salary grades.	*Administrative Science Quarterly*
Bozeman & Kingsley	1998	Risk culture in public and private organizations.	*Public Administration Review*
Rainey & Bozeman	2000	Comparing public and private organizations: Empirical research and the power of the a priori.	*Journal of Public Administration Research and Theory*
Maitlis & Ozcelik	2004	Toxic decision processes: A study of emotion and organizational decision-making.	*Organization Science*
Chun & Rainey	2005	Goal ambiguity and organizational performance in US federal agencies.	*Journal of Public Administration Research and Theory*
Sarasvathy et al.	2008	Designing organizations that design environments: Lessons from entrepreneurial expertise.	*Organization Studies*

Author	Year	Title	Journal
Lee, Rainey, & Chun	2009	Of politics and purpose: Political salience and goal ambiguity of US federal agencies.	Public Administration
Stazyk & Goerdel	2011	The benefits of bureaucracy: Public managers' perceptions of political support, goal ambiguity, and organizational effectiveness.	Journal of Public Administration Research and Theory
Jung	2014a	Extending the theory of goal ambiguity to programs: Examining the relationship between goal ambiguity and performance.	Public Administration Review
Jung	2014b	Organizational goal ambiguity and job satisfaction in the public sector.	Journal of Public Administration Research and Theory
Jung	2014c	Why are goals important in the public sector? Exploring the benefits of goal clarity for reducing turnover intention.	Journal of Public Administration Research and Theory
Davis & Stazyk	2015	Developing and testing a new goal taxonomy: Accounting for the complexity of ambiguity and political support.	Journal of Public Administration Research and Theory
Rainey & Jung	2015	A conceptual framework for analysis of goal ambiguity in public organizations.	Journal of Public Administration Research and Theory
Gonzalez-Mulé et al.	2016	Channeled autonomy: The joint effects of autonomy and feedback on team performance through organizational goal clarity.	Journal of Management

Table 1 (cont.)

Author	Year	Article title	Journal
Lee & Hageman	2018	Talk the talk or walk the walk? An examination of sustainability accounting implementation.	*Journal of Business Ethics*
		Category ambiguity	
		• Ambiguity associated with organizational labels, new markets, or organizations • Normally impacting the capacity to evaluate an organization and its value • Recent work on ambiguity as a desirable and stable feature of the category	
Fleischer	2009	Ambiguity and the equity of rating systems: United States brokerage firms, 1995–2000.	*Administrative Science Quarterly*
Pontikes	2012	Two sides of the same coin: How ambiguous classification affects multiple audiences' evaluations.	*Administrative Science Quarterly*
Bartel & Wiesenfeld	2013	The social negotiation of group prototype ambiguity in dynamic organizational contexts.	*Academy of Management Review*
Granqvist, Grodal, & Woolley	2013	Hedging your bets: Explaining executives' market labeling strategies in nanotechnology.	*Organization Science*
Wang & Jensen	2019	A bridge too far: Divestiture as a strategic reaction to status inconsistency.	*Management Science*
Chliova, Mair, & Vernis	2020	Persistent category ambiguity: The case of social entrepreneurship.	*Organization Studies*
Boghossian & David	2021	Under the umbrella: Goal-derived category construction and product category nesting.	*Administrative Science Quarterly*
Boulongne & Durand	2021	Evaluating ambiguous offerings.	*Organization Science*

important role of leaders – both current and emergent – in regulating and modeling emotional reactions to contextual ambiguity (Bridwell-Mitchell, 2016; Pescosolido, 2002; Wolbers, Boersma, & Groenewegen, 2018).

A specific stream of literature has focused on selected organizational environments as sites of structural ambiguity. This is the case of knowledge intensive firms, defined by Alvesson as ambiguity-intensive, because ambiguities characterize "their claimed core product (knowledge), what they are doing (working with knowledge) and the results of their work" (1993: 1006–1007). To manage such ambiguities, organizational members rely on the power of image and talk (Alvesson, 2001; Alvesson & Sveningsson, 2003). At the same time the strong organizational culture characterizing knowledge-intensive firms, based on an acceptance of ambiguity, can promote the development of a loyal and effective workforce (Robertson & Swan, 2003).

4.2.2 Information Ambiguity

Information ambiguity can be seen, if interpreted in a broad manner, as a basic form of uncertainty. However, it is useful not to regard all lack of information or knowledge as information ambiguity, but rather to focus on the multiple interpretations or meanings of such information or knowledge. Information ambiguity, also discussed as information equivocality, has been defined by Daft and Macintosh (1981: 211) as the "multiplicity of meaning conveyed by information about organizational activities" and as information that allows for "different and conflicting interpretations about the work context." Pich, Loch, and Meyer (2002) define general information inadequacy as caused by information uncertainty (not enough is known), ambiguity (the causal links of information are unclear), and complexity.

Equivocal information is generally a major problem in organizations and firms. If information lends itself to conflicting interpretations made by several people, the consequences can be harmful. Daft and Lengel (1986) elaborate why and how organizations process information and look at structural processes that aim to clarify ambiguity constantly, like regular team meetings, formal reports, surveys and studies, and special departments. Schwenk (1988) suggests that devil's advocacy helps decision-makers confront assumptions based on ambiguous information and Moussavi and Evans (1993) agree with previous scholars that to avoid ambiguity shared schemata facilitate shared understandings/interpretation of information in an organization, but also argue that more effort must be put into achieving converged interpretations (or coherent information among individuals in an organization).

4.2.3 Causal Ambiguity

Causal ambiguity deals with the incapacity to fully understand the link between causes and effects in the functioning of an organization and the achievements of results. It can be defined as a lack of clarity in how the "actions and results, inputs and outcomes, or competencies and advantages are linked" (Konlechner & Ambrosini, 2019: 2353). Thus, it can be seen as a core element in decision-making, usually as a key problem or challenge hampering effective decisions or action.

In the organizational context, causal ambiguity has played a key role in studies of competitive advantage and performance. This is especially the case with the resource-based view (RBV). One of the early arguments was made by Lippman and Rumelt (1982), who developed the concept of causal ambiguity to explain how firms generate profits in perfect competition. In their view, causal ambiguity explains superior performance as it protects specific firms from imitation. Thus, in the RBV context causal ambiguity has been seen as a key part of competitive advantage; for example, Barney (1991) has explained how causal ambiguity is a source of competitive advantage if the managers involved do not fully understand the links between their resources and performance.

Two types of causal ambiguity have since been identified: linkage ambiguity and characteristic ambiguity (King & Zeithaml, 2001). Linkage ambiguity is created by decision-makers and regards the link between competency and competitive advantage. Characteristic ambiguity is a lack of clarity regarding the resources and competencies themselves; for example, tacit knowledge about an organization's resources or cultural values that are not explicitly known. Ambrosini and Bowman (2010) supplement this categorization by arguing that linkage ambiguity is really about the "perceived ambiguity" between resources and performance; this ambiguity can be caused by characteristic ambiguity (which results when managers do not understand how complex resources work) or by faults in management.

A recent review (Konlechner & Ambrosini, 2019) lists three major ways causal ambiguity is discussed in research: (1) as an interfirm barrier to imitation, (2) as an intrafirm barrier to factor mobility, and (3) as a trigger for intrafirm learning. While causal ambiguity has been first discussed as an isolating factor that prevents imitation, it has since been related more to knowledge transfer and organizational learning. Thus, there is ongoing debate about whether causal ambiguity is beneficial to a company or organization by making its processes inimitable (because not even management understands its success) or whether it makes effective handling of resources or knowledge transfer impossible (McEvily, Das, & McCabe, 2000; Reed & DeFillippi, 1990; Szulanski, Cappetta, & Jensen, 2004).

Causal ambiguity can also contribute to the survival of harmful and or unethical practices in firms and organizations (Vermeulen, 2018).

4.2.4 Goal Ambiguity

Goal ambiguity refers to the inability of an organization to fully define its goals, objectives, or targets. It implies unclarity in the objectives (of the organization) and the "future state of the organization" or its projects (Chun & Rainey, 2005: 531). Goal ambiguity can be seen in the early models of organizational decision-making, where it is defined as multiple, changing, and alternative goals (Cohen, March, & Olsen, 1972; Cyert & March, 1963; March & Simon, 1958). However, there is a more recent stream of research that focuses on goal ambiguity and details its various dimensions and aspects. For instance, Chun and Rainey (2005) identify four types of goal ambiguity: mission comprehension ambiguity (the understandability of the mission statement), directive goal ambiguity (the directives and actions that should be taken to reach goals), evaluative goal ambiguity (evaluation of progress toward a goal – e.g. performance indicators), and priority goal ambiguity (prioritizing multiple goals to achieve larger goals or prioritizing goals hierarchically). By contrast, Jung (2014a, 2014b, 2014c) offers another typology: target ambiguity, timeline ambiguity, and evaluation ambiguity.

There is a general understanding that public sector organizations have much higher goal ambiguity than their counterparts in the private sector (e.g., Schramm, 1975; Turcotte, 1974). Studies have since added nuance to this understanding. Rainey and Bozeman (2000: 452) show that public managers do not acknowledge problems caused by goal ambiguity and Stazyk and Goerdel (2011) argue that high levels of hierarchical authority can offset goal ambiguity in public organizations. Factors like high political salience/visibility can translate to higher levels of goal ambiguity in public organizations (Lee, Rainey, & Chun, 2009), while budgets that prioritize some projects over others can provide workers with better goal clarity and improve their motivation (Shon et al., 2020). Additionally, if workers receive generous feedback (Gonzalez-Mulé et al., 2016) and perceive their job as important (Jung, 2014a), they are more likely to experience goal clarity.

4.2.5 Category Ambiguity

Categories are cognitive representations or classifications that simplify the information burden associated with making sense of social phenomena (Durand & Boulongne, 2017). Categorization has been traditionally seen as a means to alleviate ambiguity around social phenomena by increasing familiarity and resemblance. Category research has incorporated the study of ambiguity from two perspectives: ambiguity in categorization processes (Pontikes, 2012), where organizations ambiguously signal their membership in a market category or display multiple memberships (Zuckerman, 1999); and the emergence of ambiguous categories themselves, defined as categories for which multiple divergent frames exist (Chliova, Mair, & Vernis, 2020: 1021).

Most work in this area focuses on market categories and zooms in on the ambiguity of the positioning of an organization/firm in a market category. Market labels and categories, for example "healthcare" or "construction," are shared reference points that influence how stakeholders conceive of and act toward an organization (Granqvist, Grodal, & Woolley, 2013). While some research (Granqvist, Grodal, & Woolley, 2013; Zuckerman, 1999, 2000) has shown that firms face difficulty if they are associated with several market categories simultaneously, most authors appear to agree that category ambiguity can be advantageous (Chliova, Mair, & Vernis, 2020; Fleischer, 2009; Pontikes, 2012). However, this ambiguity has to be managed and engineered. For example, a hedging strategy – at times associating the organization with one category and at other times rejecting it and relating to another, thereby identifying with more than one market – can be used to widen the organization/firm's scope (Granqvist, Grodal, & Woolley, 2013). More specifically, Granqvist, Grodal, and Woolley (2013) stress the importance and difficulty of market labeling in nascent markets where existing labels do not exist. Pontikes (2012) argues that ambiguous market labels are unappealing and confusing for consumers who are market-takers, but can appeal to venture capitalists who are market-makers. Boulongne and Durand (2021) explore how audiences themselves partake in product categorization and show that a different approach by an audience (e.g., goal-based categorization) leads to a more favorable view of ambiguous products. Wang and Jensen (2019) in turn discuss identity ambiguity and elaborate on the challenges faced by firms in seeking to present coherent market identities. Thus, managing category ambiguity can also involve aspects of strategic ambiguity, which we will turn to next.

5 Strategic Perspectives: Discursively Constructed Strategic Ambiguity

The purpose of this section is to offer an overview of more recent and strategic perspectives on ambiguity. These strategic perspectives focus on ambiguity that is discursively constructed to achieve strategic purposes. This view originally built upon the work of Eisenberg (Eisenberg, 1984; Eisenberg, Goodall, &

Trethewey, 2013; Eisenberg & Riley, 1988; Eisenberg & Witten, 1987) in communication studies, but has since spread to the field of organization and management theory, more specifically to studies of strategy-making and organizational change.

5.1 Seminal Research on Discursively Constructed Strategic Ambiguity: The Work of Eric Eisenberg

In the organization and management literature, a turning point in the conceptualization of ambiguity occurred in the 1980s via the work of Eric M. Eisenberg and colleagues (Eisenberg, 1984; Eisenberg & Witten, 1987). Their work, originally in communication studies, marks a shift from conceiving ambiguity as an abstract condition permeating much of organizational life and especially decision-making processes to conceiving it as discursively constructed by "individuals" who "use ambiguity purposefully to accomplish their goals" (Eisenberg, 1984: 231). In his research, Eisenberg was the first to use the term "strategic ambiguity" to indicate the intentional construction and use of ambiguity in communication within and around organizations. He argues that ambiguity is as least as useful to organizational members as clarity, or sometimes even more (Eisenberg & Witten, 1987). Hence his seminal contributions reverse the prevalent view of ambiguity as problematic for organizations, both internally (e.g., Denis et al., 2011; Hennestad, 1990) and externally (e.g., Allen, 1958), and also point to the need to account more generally for the positive returns of ambiguity for managers and organizations.

Since then, the concept of strategic ambiguity has not only become part of communication theory (Eisenberg, Goodall, & Trethewey, 2013) and employed frequently in communication studies (e.g., Contractor & Ehrlich, 1993; Markham, 1996; Paul & Strbiak, 1997; Wexler, 2009). It has also inspired a stream of studies in strategy (e.g., Abdallah & Langley, 2014), organization studies (e.g., Cappellaro, Compagni, & Vaara, 2021), and ethics (e.g., Guthey & Morsing, 2014; Scandelius & Cohen, 2016). All these studies embrace the strategic perspective on ambiguity proposed by Eisenberg and employ the very concept of strategic ambiguity.

5.1.1 Ambiguous Language versus Ambiguous Communication

In his 1984 seminal paper, Eisenberg is adamant that strategic ambiguity is not "an attribute of messages," but rather something that develops through the act of communicating and is therefore "a *relational* variable which arises through a combination of source, message, and receiver factors" (Eisenberg, 1984: 229;

emphasis in the original). In doing so, Eisenberg strives to shift the attention of scholars away from the analysis of ambiguous language that lacks specific detail or is abstract, arguing that the "particular message strategy chosen" by the source of the message is not "equivalent to whether an individual has been relatively clear or ambiguous" (1984: 231). In this sense, Eisenberg suggests that detailed and specific language can generate ambiguity as much as imprecise and figurative language. He in fact urges scholars to explore the ambiguity of meaning created in the relationship between the actors (source and receiver) exchanging a message. In his words, the degree of strategic ambiguity in organizational communication depends in the end on "the degree to which a source has narrowed the possible interpretations of a message and succeeded in achieving a correspondence between his or her intentions and the interpretation of the receiver" (Eisenberg, 1984: 231).

Eisenberg envisages many instances in organizational life in which the source of a message (often a manager) would *intentionally* avoid achieving correspondence between intent and the interpretation of receivers, mainly employees. According to this perspective, ambiguity is therefore not only something inherent in organizational life and phenomena as the intrinsic view suggests (March & Olsen, 1976), but engendered in the plurality of interpretations allowed by organizational talk and communication. While Eisenberg mainly stresses the intentionality of organizational actors in creating ambiguity, he never excludes the possibility that ambiguity can be created inadvertently and merely used strategically, that is, to accomplish goals. Giroux (2006) subsequently shows that while ambiguity around quality management is discursively constructed at the field level with little collective intention, the increasing multiplicity of meanings associated with it has facilitated widespread diffusion of this management practice across the world.

5.1.2 Theoretical Origins and Cross-Fertilizations

Eisenberg roots his conceptualization of ambiguity in organizational symbolism (Dandridge, Mitroff, & Joyce, 1980; Pfeffer, 1981). This theoretical take proposes to conceive of organizations as imbued with symbols, that is, objects, actions, and language conveying abstract meanings, making the "political, dramaturgical, and language skills" of managers more important than their analytical and cognitive capacities (Eisenberg, 1984; Pfeffer, 1981). Based on this perspective, strategic ambiguity could be seen as one of the instruments at the disposal of managers to allow multiple interpretations of the same symbol by employees in an organization (Eisenberg, 1984; Eisenberg & Riley, 1988).

Despite organizational symbolism being the main theoretical foundation of Eisenberg's seminal papers, references to the work of Karl Weick are also present in his papers. In a later essay (Eisenberg, 2007), he indeed acknowledges how Weick, by emphasizing the contingency of organizational life and the relevance of communication and talk in organizations (Weick, 1984), has been aligned with the interpretive turn in the field of communication studies (Putnam & Pacanowsky, 1983). In addition, Weick's pioneering work on the role of equivocality – as in the plurality of interpretations – for (effective) organizing appears to conform to a large extent to Eisenberg's conceptualization of strategic ambiguity and diverge, for instance, from the predominant views on the need for shared meanings and consensus in effective organizing.

Finally, in conceptualizing strategic ambiguity, Eisenberg does not neglect to draw connections with the fields of political science (Edelman, 1977) and international relations from which he takes examples of the use of ambiguity mainly in the communication of goals. These references confirm the political nature that Eisenberg attributes to the creation and use of ambiguity in communication in and around organizations. Indeed, reference to studies in political science are also present in subsequent studies (e.g., Gioia, Nag, & Corley, 2012; Sillince, Jarzabkowski, & Shaw, 2012). These papers explicitly draw parallels between how political candidates (Glazer, 1990; Page, 1976; Shepsle, 1972) or political actors (Padgett & Ansell, 1993; Ring & Perry, 1985) maintain ambiguity around their goals and actions in order to win elections or build alliances and how managers ambiguously communicate their vision of organizational change or of a new strategy to employees.

5.1.3 Purposes of Strategic Ambiguity

Strategic ambiguity can serve several purposes in organizations. Eisenberg and colleagues (Eisenberg, 1984; Eisenberg, Goodall, & Trethewey, 2013) distinguish three main sets of purposes that can be achieved by creating or using ambiguity: (a) promoting "unified diversity" within organizations and with external and diverse stakeholders or audiences; (b) facilitating organizational change, and (c) preserving "privileged positions."

As to the first purpose, Eisenberg points that ambiguous language can facilitate multiple interpretations of the same message and hence flexibility, and thanks to a "level of abstraction at which agreement *can* occur" (Eisenberg, 1984: 233, emphasis in the original) at the same time provide some level of healthy consensus across diverse actors. In this sense, strategic ambiguity can reduce conflict and allow actors with divergent views to speak "with one voice." In contrast, the second purpose focuses on the capacity of strategic ambiguity – mainly around goals – to promote organizational change by allowing organizational members to preserve a sense of continuity while simultaneously adapting to the shifting nature of goals during the change process. Eisenberg also points to the fact that ambiguity promotes development of interpersonal relationships. When an individual conveys ambiguous goals in a message to either an internal or an external audience, the recipients tend to interpret the goals in their own terms. They perceive affinity with the sender and are inclined to establish a collaborative relationship.

Finally, Eisenberg points to the possibility of using strategic ambiguity to avoid compromising with explicit messages positions of consolidated credibility, in order to preserve temporal advantages over competitors or maintain control over interorganizational collaboration by preserving the possibility to withdraw from a partnership without "losing face" (Eisenberg, 1984; Eisenberg, Goodall, & Trethewey, 2013). Eisenberg suggests that ambiguous communication can achieve all this because it can be more easily rejected by organizations than clearer messages. Asserting something ambiguously and then leaving the entire burden of interpretation to the receiver allow organizations to dismiss all those interpretations that may threaten it, and hence exercise a form of control or power over the receiver.

Eisenberg and Witten (1987) dedicate a large part of their seminal paper to explain that ambiguous communication and organizational secrecy, that is, the extent to which organizations conceal information about their activities and strategies from internal or external audiences, are closely linked. They suggest that overly disclosive communication may be detrimental to organizations in many instances such as crises or collective bargaining negotiations, but that, most importantly, it does not eliminate power asymmetries between organizations or between managers and subordinates within organizations.

5.2 Organizational Scholarship on Discursively Constructed Strategic Ambiguity

In what follows, we focus on the main streams of literature on discursively constructed ambiguity that have been inspired by the work of Eisenberg and colleagues. We especially zoom in on three perspectives that we label conceptual ambiguity, rhetorical ambiguity, and narrative and frame ambiguity. All these closely related approaches examine how various forms of language use can be used to create, maintain, or reduce ambiguity. Conceptual ambiguity means ambiguity created by specific words or linguistic devices that can be interpreted in different ways. Rhetorical ambiguity denotes the deliberate use of language to influence others' understanding of specific organizational phenomena or issues. Narrative and frame ambiguity in turn imply existence of multiple narratives or different frames around an issue. Table 2 presents the main types of discursively constructed ambiguity and provides further reading, listing sample references. The table also details the organizational processes affected by ambiguity.

5.2.1 Conceptual Ambiguity

The first stream of work examines how language generates linguistic ambiguity (Nicolai & Dautwiz, 2010), equivocal language (Denis et al., 2011), or linguistic equivocality (Abdallah & Langley, 2014). In such conceptual ambiguity, ambiguity is generated by the use of single words or keywords and refers to how certain specific words in a text are used in relation to a variety of different descriptors (Abdallah & Langley, 2014; Jalonen, Schildt, & Vaara, 2018). In this perspective, keywords are not only highly salient words within a discourse that are closely associated with issues central to that discourse, but also have multiple meanings. Ambiguity is thus generated by the semantic openness of the concepts. For example, Leitch and Davenport (2007) analyze how the word "sustainability" was used within a set of documents intended by the New Zealand Government to guide development of biotechnology and the role that usage of this word played in facilitating coherent presentation of a change message. In a complimentary vein, Meyer and Höllerer defined CSR as an ambiguous term with a "complexity-neutralizing capacity" (2016: 382). Similarly, Abdallah and Langley's (2014) study of strategy planning in a cultural organization illuminates the frequent and equivocal use of the word "relevance" appearing in association with a variety of other objects and expressions. The word is used in a vague manner to refer to the organization as a whole, but also more specifically to the organization's production program.

Analyses of the single words and keywords also characterize the studies on management fashions, that is, abstract, often vague and fuzzily defined, sometimes also contradictory concepts. Giroux's (2006) study on total quality management (TQM) is based on analysis of texts containing selected terms such as "total quality management," "total quality," or "quality circles." Similar arguments apply to the concepts of business process reengineering (Benders & Van Veen, 2001) or core competence framework (Nicolai & Dautwiz, 2010).

A distinguishing feature of conceptual ambiguity is its intertextual component. This means that ambiguity is generated not by an individual word in a single instance, but rather by its use across texts and time. Many of these studies therefore uncover patterns of semantic use of words by analyzing a series of texts, for example, in the form of documents, print press, or interview

Table 2 Organizational scholarship on discursively constructed strategic ambiguity, by type and year

Author	Year	Article title	Journal
		Conceptual ambiguity	
		• Ambiguity generated by a single word or keyword that is used in relation to a variety of different descriptors	
Benders & Van Veen	2001	What's in a fashion? Interpretative viability and management fashions.	*Organization*
Giroux	2006	"It was such a handy term": Management fashions and pragmatic ambiguity.	*Journal of Management Studies*
Leitch & Davenport	2007	Strategic ambiguity as a discourse practice: The role of keywords in the discourse on "sustainable" biotechnology.	*Discourse Studies*
Nicolai & Dautwiz	2010	Fuzziness in action: What consequences has the linguistic ambiguity of the core competence concept for organizational usage?	*British Journal of Management*
Denis et al.	2011	Escalating indecision: Between reification and strategic ambiguity.	*Organization Science*
Abdallah & Langley	2014	The double edge of ambiguity in strategic planning.	*Journal of Management Studies*
Meyer & Höllerer	2016	Laying a smoke screen: Ambiguity and neutralization as strategic responses to intra-institutional complexity.	*Strategic Organization*
Jalonen, Schildt, & Vaara	2018	Strategic concepts as micro-level tools in strategic sensemaking.	*Strategic Management Journal*
		Rhetorical ambiguity	
		• Ambiguity constructed through the use of metaphors, analogy, irony, or other rhetorical means	
		• Includes also absence of speech, that is, silence	

Author	Year	Title	Journal
Kelemen	2000	Too much or too little ambiguity: The language of total quality management.	*Journal of Management Studies*
Leitch & Davenport	2002	Strategic ambiguity in communicating public sector change.	*Journal of Communication Management*
Van Dyne, Ang, & Botero	2003	Conceptualizing employee silence and employee voice as multidimensional constructs.	*Journal of Management Studies*
Ramsay	2004	Trope control: The costs and benefits of metaphor unreliability in the description of empirical phenomena.	*British Journal of Management*
Jarzabkowski, Sillince, & Shaw	2010	Strategic ambiguity as a rhetorical resource for enabling multiple interests.	*Human Relations*
Sillince, Jarzabkowski, & Shaw	2012	Shaping strategic action through the rhetorical construction and exploitation of ambiguity.	*Organization Science*
Spee & Jarzabkowski	2017	Agreeing on what? Creating joint accounts of strategic change.	*Organization Science*
Sorsa & Vaara	2020	How can pluralistic organizations proceed with strategic change? A processual account of rhetorical contestation, convergence, and partial agreement in a Nordic city organization.	*Organization Science*

Table 2 (cont.)

Author	Year	Article title	Journal
Cappellaro, Compagni, & Vaara	2021	Maintaining strategic ambiguity for protection: Struggles over opacity, equivocality, and absurdity around the Sicilian Mafia.	*Academy of Management Journal*
Narrative and frame ambiguity			
• Ambiguity linked with multiple narratives around organizations or using different frames around an issue			
• Often associated with the emergence of new issues stimulating sensemaking efforts			
Sonenshein	2010	We're changing – Or are we? Untangling the role of progressive, regressive, and stability narratives during strategic change implementation.	*Academy of Management Journal*
Cappelen & Strandgaard Pedersen	2021	Inventing culinary heritage through strategic historical ambiguity.	*Organization Studies*
Feront & Bertels	2021	The impact of frame ambiguity on field-level change.	*Organization Studies*
Impacts: Strategic change			
• Ambiguity might lead to (mostly) positive outcomes in strategy-making or strategic change			
• Boundary conditions apply			
Markham	1996	Designing discourse: A critical analysis of strategic ambiguity and workplace control.	*Management Communication Quarterly*
Sewell & Barker	2006	Coercion versus care: Using irony to make sense of organizational surveillance.	*Academy Management Review*

| Aggerholm, Asmuß, & Thomsen | 2012 | The role of recontextualization in the multivocal, ambiguous process of strategizing. | Journal of Management Inquiry |
| Gioia, Nag, & Corley | 2012 | Visionary ambiguity and strategic change: The virtue of vagueness in launching major organizational change. | Journal of Management Inquiry |

Articles already cited above: Denis et al., 2011; Feront & Bertels, 2021; Jarzabkowski, Sillince, & Shaw, 2010; Kelemen, 2000; Sillince, Jarzabkowski, & Shaw, 2012; Sonenshein, 2010; Sorsa & Vaara, 2020; Spee & Jarzabkowski, 2017

Impacts: Stakeholder relationship management

- Strategically ambiguous discourse is employed to communicate change efforts to external stakeholders
- Ambiguity strategically used to protect organizations from negative outside evaluations and the potential harmful effects of public scrutiny

Sellnow & Ulmer	1995	Ambiguous argument as advocacy in organizational crisis communication.	Argumentation and Advocacy
Ulmer & Sellnow	1997	Strategic ambiguity and the ethic of significant choice in the tobacco industry's crisis communication.	Communication Studies
Paul & Strbiak	1997	The ethics of strategic ambiguity.	The Journal of Business Communication
Ulmer & Sellnow	2000	Consistent questions of ambiguity in organizational crisis communication: Jack in the Box as a case study.	Journal of Business Ethics
Davenport & Leitch	2005	Circuits of power in practice: Strategic ambiguity as delegation of authority.	Organization Studies
Wexler	2009	Strategic ambiguity in emergent coalitions: The triple bottom line.	Corporate Communications: An International Journal

Table 2 (cont.)

Author	Year	Article title	Journal
Guthey & Morsing	2014	CSR and the mediated emergence of strategic ambiguity.	*Journal of Business Ethics*
Scandelius & Cohen	2016	Achieving collaboration with diverse stakeholders: The role of strategic ambiguity in CSR communication.	*Journal of Business Research*

Articles already cited above: Cappellaro, Compagni, & Vaara, 2021; Leitch & Davenport, 2002 transcripts. When studying texts issued by the *same actor(s)* over time, use of the same equivocal word, for example, "sustainability" or "relevance," allows different texts to signal an internal and intertextual coherence and facilitates an inclusive voice. This was shown by Leitch and Davenport (2007) in their analysis of the intertextual chain that linked five major policy documents released by the New Zealand Government between 2001 and 2003 that were intended to drive significant social change. Alternatively, authors of texts can generate ambiguity by adding or deleting words across texts. For example, Denis et al. (2011) show how initial versions of a merger principle about the configuration of services on each of the sites provided more detail than the final version. Details were deliberately removed to allow people to sign in comfort.

When studying texts produced by *different actors*, ambiguity is instead generated by "interpretive viability" (Benders & Van Veen, 2001) characterizing the individual words and constructs. The study of management fashions, in particular, shows how the conceptual ambiguity of the words and associated constructs allows different managers to "eclectically select those elements that appeal to them," interpret them as the fashion's core idea, or opportunistically select those suitable to their purposes. At the organizational level, different actors may interpret a concept differently. This has been shown by Nicolai and Dautwiz (2010), who trace how interpretations of the definition of core competences and the notion of what the company's core competences actually are vary greatly. In other words, as they argue, ambiguity has two sides; it depends on both the conceptual ambiguity of the original text and the contextual ambiguity of the adopting organization (Nicolai & Dautwiz, 2010).

5.2.2 Rhetorical Ambiguity

A second set of studies focuses on rhetoric, which is a branch of discourse and language theory associated with persuasion, as a theoretical and methodological lens for understanding how multiple actors construct strategic ambiguity to influence different audiences.

In continuity with the conceptual ambiguity described above, scholars have studied how specific *figures of speech* generate ambiguity. The most common one is the metaphor, a figure of speech typically based on the transfer of meaning from a source domain to a target domain. As defined by Richards (1936), "when we use a metaphor we have two thoughts of different things active together and supported by a single word or phrase whose meaning is a result of their interaction. We arrive at [the meaning] only through the interpretative possibilities of the whole utterance." Metaphors are open to multiple interpretations and therefore provide interpretive room within which stakeholders may engage with an organization. Metaphors, however, are not entirely open; they instead carry with them associations that have been built up through common usage. Leitch and Davenport (2002) study how the major science-funding agency in New Zealand deployed new metaphors and the investment metaphor specifically, as a central element of its communication with external stakeholders during a change process. Similarly, Kelemen (2000) analyzes the concept of total quality management in four organizations. She focuses on three properties of language – labels, metaphors, and platitudes – and argues that while labels and platitudes are used to instill a sense of order, metaphors are used with the opposite purpose, that of increasing ambiguity by inviting multiple and diverse interpretations. Ambiguity is generated by both the structure of the metaphor and the way in which it generates meaning in the mind of the reader. As Ramsay noted in an examination of the supply-chain metaphor in business circles, using metaphors for strategic purposes may not be an easy process because "the linguistic images in the metaphor interact with the reader's personal knowledge and experiences and the cognitive structures formed in this process will be different for each reader" (2004: 145).

The study of rhetoric in relation to strategic ambiguity has also been the focus of a series of studies by Jarzabkowski and colleagues (Jarzabkowski, Sillince, & Shaw, 2010; Sillince, Jarzabkowski, & Spee, 2012; see also Spee & Jarzabkowski, 2017). In their analysis of the internationalization strategy within a business school, Sillince, Jarzabkowski, and Spee (2012) show how actors use rhetoric to construct different types of ambiguity – protective, invitational, and adaptive – in order to support the interests of both academic and managerial sides. In another study (2010), they identify different rhetorical positions based on the degree of broadness or narrowness of the articulation of an ambiguous goal and on the range of stakeholders' interests and show how each of these uses ambiguity in strategic action. More complex rhetorical arguments have also been found to generate ambiguity. Sorsa and Vaara (2020) identify the central role of *consensus arguments*, that is, arguments that involve a rhetorical syllogism called "enthymemes" characterized by concealment of the value premises. In their study of a Nordic city organization, the authors noted how arguments that left the underlying assumptions implicit generated the ambiguity needed for construction of common ground in strategy texts.

Within the realm of rhetorical ambiguity, the role of nonverbal language – and silence in particular – deserves special attention in strategically creating ambiguity. Departing from a traditional view of silence as a passive act, essentially a nonbehavior, a few organizational scholars have conceptualized silence as purposeful. This perspective is rooted in communication studies, which regard interactive silence as strategic and intentional (Pinder & Harlos, 2001) and able to create ambiguity in interpersonal exchanges (Bruneau, 1973). Van Dyne, Ang, and Botero (2003) focus on ambiguity as equivocality in attributions by observers of the motives of employees based on the behavioral cues provided by their silence or voice. They suggest that silence is more ambiguous to observers than voice because it provides fewer behavioral cues. When an employee is silent, observers do not have access to speech acts, subtle speech cues, or back-channel communication cues, but only nonverbal behavior that often evokes several possible interpretations or multiple meanings and is therefore ambiguous. In a very different organizational setting, one of clandestine organizations, Cappellaro, Compagni, and Vaara (2021) also show how silence produces ambiguity in the eyes of observers. By studying the case of the Sicilian mafia, the authors show how silence is strategically employed by Mafiosi to generate ambiguity in the perception state representatives have of mafia power: that is, whether silence (as the absence of violence) should be interpreted as a signal of a weaker or more powerful mafia organization. In contrast to Van Dyne, Ang, and Botero (2003), Cappellaro, Compagni, and Vaara (2021) show how silence and speech can be deployed dynamically in order to actively foster strategic ambiguity. Organizations may in fact abandon a strategy of silence when it begins to lose its effectiveness, engage external audiences in finer speech-based strategies, and then for renewed effectiveness revert to silence in combination with other tactics. Hence, they argue that "more than a strategy of silence we should be talking about strategies of silence, deployed by organizations with different timing and impact on external audiences" (Cappellaro, Compagni, & Vaara, 2021: 24).

5.2.3 Narrative and Frame Ambiguity

A final analytical perspective focuses on how higher-order, more complex structures of a discourse can be used to create ambiguity. A *narrative* is a tool used to influence others' understandings and is an outcome of the collective construction of meaning (Sonenshein, 2010). Strategic ambiguity can reside in both the construction of the individual narrative and in the interpretation of different narratives. An example of the former is the study of Cappelen and Strandgaard Pedersen (2021) on the Turkish culinary movement, which focuses on how actors deliberately create different forms of ambiguity to legitimate historical narratives of a common cultural heritage. These forms of ambiguity concern the origin, artefacts, and ownership of the culinary movement and allow actors to (re)create a common past, while granting flexibility for future action. Ambiguity at the level of the interpretation of multiple narratives is also well exemplified by the work of Sonenshein (2010). In a study of the implementation of an organizational change initiative, he showed how managers were intentionally equivocal about the meaning of change, developing narratives that combined dialectically opposite categories of significant change (the progressive narrative) and insignificant change (stability narratives).

The notion of opposing narratives as generative of ambiguity is also echoed in studies of *frames and cognitive representations*. While intrinsic views see frames as cognitive filters to reduce contextual and information ambiguity (Hubbard et al., 2018; Sgourev, 2013) or to leverage on ambiguous issues or concepts (Hahn et al., 2014), frames can also generate ambiguity. This typically happens when framing activity includes contradictory or opposite frames (Litrico & David, 2017). Feront and Bertels (2021) investigates how the ambiguous frame employed by proponents of responsible investment influenced the interpretive dynamics of the field constituents and affected field-level change, differentiating between the degrees of ambiguity generated by each component of a frame – diagnostic, prognostic, or motivational.

5.3 How Strategic Ambiguity Informs Organizational Processes

These different forms of discursively constructed strategic ambiguity have been studied in relation to several organizational processes, shedding new light on their antecedents, dynamics, and outcomes. We focus on two broad kinds of organizational processes where strategic ambiguity has been shown to play a major role: strategic change and stakeholder relationship management.

5.3.1 Strategic Change

Strategic ambiguity can be specifically used in processes of strategic change inside an organization in contexts of potential high contestation. Two mechanisms have been identified to support this function. The first mechanism through which strategically ambiguous discourse – in the form of concepts, arguments, narratives or frames – supports change initiatives is by allowing the coexistence of divergent points of view regarding change efforts and, as a consequence, reducing opposition to change inside the organization. This is done by creating space for accommodating simultaneous multiple interpretations (Denis et al., 2011), that is, interpretations comprising multiple prevailing meanings and new meanings within a joint account (Spee & Jarzabkowski, 2017), by temporally alternating different narratives that appeal to both defenders of the status quo and supporters of the change initiative (Sonenshein, 2010), or by masking the value premises of change arguments (Sorsa & Vaara, 2020).

In conceptualizing how ambiguity relates to strategic change, specific attention has been devoted to show that ambiguity is not an exclusive resource of a single group but can instead be exploited by multiple actors during the strategic change initiative. For example, Jarzabkowski and colleagues (Jarzabkowski, Sillince, & Shaw, 2010; Sillince, Jarzabkowski, & Shaw, 2012) illuminate how collective action in change initiatives results from how different constituents adopt different types of rhetorical ambiguity over time to advance their interests (Sillince, Jarzabkowski, & Shaw, 2012). In a complimentary vein, Aggerholm, Asmuß, and Thomsen (2012) focus on the subsequent phases – strategy authoring, translation, and interpretation – of a strategizing process and show how ambiguity arises through the presence of multiple strategic actors within and across phases. In their analysis of strategy work in a Nordic city organization, Jalonen, Schildt, and Vaara (2018) in turn show how a degree of ambiguity around new strategic concepts is needed to mobilize people but how over time increasing ambiguity tends to hamper strategic decision-making. Moving at the interorganizational level, Wexler (2009) traces the process through which different loosely coupled discourse communities coalesce around an emerging coalition focused on the ambiguous concept of triple bottom line. In these streams of work, ambiguity is channeled by powerful groups but also emerges from the interaction of different constituents.

A second, deeper, mechanism through which strategic ambiguity shapes strategic change processes is by triggering a revision of the knowledge basis and forms of the organizational actors. According to this view, rather than masking divergences among organizational actors, ambiguous statements regarding the strategic change efforts and new vision generate new and divergent sensemaking (Weick, 1995). As illustrated by Gioia, Nag, and Corley (2012), during change processes organizational members challenge and question various elements of their interpretive frames. They interpret ambiguous vision statements – that is, statements characterized by lack of specificity and/or low emphasis – by developing new meanings for them and ultimately alter their activities to make them consistent with these new meanings. Divergent sensemaking triggered by strategic ambiguity and the associated revision of knowledge may ultimately sediment and modify organizational practices and routines (Gioia, Nag, & Corley, 2012).

The employment of ambiguous discourse to support strategic change initiatives has nevertheless potential downsides. On the one hand, an empirical question is "how much" ambiguity is needed for the successful backing of change initiatives. Too much or too little ambiguity may indeed be counterproductive. For example, Feront and Bertels showed how high levels of frame ambiguity hindered field-level change. High levels of frame ambiguity "allowed for a false impression of progress, inhibited material changes, and concealed differences between actors" (2021: 1136). On the other hand, the sense of positive alignment obtained by coexistence of opposite points of view may be temporary in nature. While initially facilitating the change process by allowing organizational members to push forward their respective interpretations over time, the mobilizing effects of strategic ambiguity can lead to internal contradiction (Abdallah & Langley, 2014; Denis et al., 2011). It has therefore been argued that strategic ambiguity is beneficial in launching change processes, while it is less effective in the subsequent phase of change implementation, when it is important to establish a more precise set of goals (Gioia, Nag, & Corley, 2012). Finally, strategic ambiguity could also be (mis) used to retain control over employees within existing organizational boundaries (Kelemen, 2000; Markham, 1996; Sewell & Barker, 2006). Managers may deliberately allow ambiguity "in order to make space for manipulation" because by "keeping ambiguity in play it is the subordinates who carry the risk of blame for misinterpreting the messages" (Munro, 1995, cited in Kelemen, 2020: 492).

5.3.2 Stakeholder Relationship Management

Strategic ambiguity can also be used to manage the relationship between the organization and its external audiences. In continuity with the change dynamics described in the previous section, strategically ambiguous discourse is employed to *communicate change efforts* to external stakeholders. At the first level, ambiguity in such circumstances empowers stakeholders by allowing them to co-create meaning within organizational discourse (Scandelius & Cohen, 2016). However, such co-creation is typically guided by the organization itself, which orchestrates the degree of discursive closure and hence of participation by external stakeholders. As argued by Davenport and Leitch (2005), ambiguity is a powerful resource held by an organization "to potentially select discursive openness as an alternative to discursive closure, depending on whether they seek creative engagement with, or compliance from, their stakeholders." Ambiguity is thus seen as "a form of authority delegation for creative stakeholder engagement" (Davenport & Leitch, 2005:1604). In addition to enabling multiple interpretations about the direction of change to coexist, strategic ambiguity provides the organization with the time to prepare for change and put into place the internal structures necessary to support such change. As Leitch and Davenport illustrated, ambiguous language provides "the time and interpretive space for an organization to develop fully its policies and procedures internally while still clearly signaling to external stakeholders the goals of change and the outcomes that were sought" (2002: 133).

Mediators can also intervene in the relationship between the organization and its stakeholders. The media for example, as illustrated by a study of CSR press coverage in Denmark (Guthey & Morsing, 2014), can further accentuate a lack of clarity regarding specific concepts, thus amplifying the degree of discursive openness. Hence strategic ambiguity can emerge from the interaction of loosely coupled groups or coalitions across organizational boundaries mediated through the business press.

A second core function of strategic ambiguity for stakeholder management is to protect organizations from negative outside evaluations and the potential harmful effects of public scrutiny. For example, Meyer and Höllerer (2016) show how expressing commitment to the ambiguous CSR concept allowed organizations that had been committed to the preexisting shareholder value model to maintain legitimacy. This function is typically performed in crisis contexts to maintain a high engagement by stakeholders with divergent interests. Here ambiguous arguments are used as advocacy tools (Sellnow & Ulmer, 1995; Ulmer & Sellnow, 1997, 2000) and display different apologetic reformative strategies (Ware & Linkugel, 1973). Such strategies include, for example, denial – which refers to the "disavowal by the leaders of any relationship with the sources of the crises" – and bolstering, which is the opposite of denial and refers to "the leaders' efforts to involve themselves with facts, objects or relationships which are viewed favorably by the audience" (Sellnow & Ulmer, 1995: 139). In their study on the public arguments developed by the leaders of Jack in the Box, a fast-food chain suspected of having caused an outbreak of *E. coli*, Sellnow and Ulmer (1995; Ulmer & Sellnow, 2000) show how leaders deployed both strategies to maintain legitimacy with stakeholders with divergent views – that is, the general public who had an interest in seeing that the organization had put in place all measures to respond to the crisis and the shareholders who were interested in claiming that the organization was not connected with the crisis.

In contexts of crises – when potential loss of legitimacy or other negative organizational repercussions are at stake – the use of strategic ambiguity gives rise to questions of its ethical implications for diverse stakeholders (Paul & Strbiak, 1997). Eisenberg, Goodall, and Trethewey (2013) argue that a focus on strategic ambiguity in organizations minimizes the importance of ethics and is used to escape blame. Elaborating on the link between strategic ambiguity and ethics, scholars contend that strategic ambiguity does not raise ethical considerations when it "poses alternative views that are based on complete and unbiased data that aims to inform" (Ulmer & Sellnow, 1997: 217). On the contrary, strategic ambiguity is unethical when it serves to obscure the sensemaking abilities of stakeholders by using biased or incomplete information

(Ulmer & Sellnow, 1997, 2000). Ulmer and Sellnow (1997) show how managers of the tobacco industry deliberately engaged in strategic ambiguity to limit the deliberative ability of external stakeholders by providing them with incomplete and biased information.

The emphasis on the use of ambiguity to protect organizations from negative outside evaluations and the ethical consequence of such use introduces the third function of strategic ambiguity, which is supporting stakeholder management by specific categories of clandestine or even criminal organizations (Cappellaro, Compagni, & Vaara, 2021). These organizations represent an extreme case of actors relying on strategic ambiguity to escape blame and display two distinctive features that differentiate them from traditional contexts of organizational change or crises. First, while in the more conventional organizations ambiguity is deployed as temporary strategy, it is essential for the survival of clandestine and criminal organizations hiding from public scrutiny. Hence, strategic ambiguity constitutes a long-term organizational strategy. Furthermore, while the aim of ambiguity during crises or change efforts is to foster consensus, clandestine and criminal organizations use strategic ambiguity to create an antagonist relationship with the scrutinizing external stakeholders. As shown in the study on the strategic use of ambiguity by the Sicilian mafia (Cappellaro, Compagni, & Vaara, 2021), as an external audience makes progress in trying to dissipate ambiguity, the organization switches strategy and ultimately shifts to a different type of ambiguity, thus aiming to keep stakeholders in a persistent state of confusion regarding its activities and strategies.

6 Trajectories in the Study of Ambiguity in Organization Theory and Future Perspectives

Based on what we have presented in the previous two sections, we identify three dimensions that characterize ambiguity differently across intrinsic and strategic perspectives: the ontological nature of ambiguity (intrinsic to organizational reality vs. socially constructed), the degree of dynamism involved (static vs. dynamic), and the sources of the phenomenon (external vs. internal origins). We first summarize these three dimensions and then elaborate on two trajectories for future research.

First, intrinsic perspectives construe ambiguity as given and structural to organizational reality, often associated with "events" and "circumstances" – such as organizational change (e.g., Srivastava, 2015) – or with "contexts" characterized by complexity and uncertainty (Stone & Brush, 1996) that provide unclear goals (Denis, Langley, & Cazale, 1996) or uncertain information environments (Forbes, 2007). Here ambiguity is linked with the cognitive acts of organizational members in interpreting situations, signals, and cues, and hence informs their decisions. In contrast, more recent studies see ambiguity as socially constructed through discursive and rhetorical processes. Hence ambiguity is not to be found in reality per se, but emerges instead through interaction (e.g., Jarzabkowski, Sillince, & Shaw, 2010). As indicated above, the literature on categories has moved from portraying ambiguity as inherently detrimental to a category to uncovering how it is actively constructed in order to avoid excessive competition or gain the support of investors (Chliova, Mair, & Vernis, 2020; Granqvist, Grodal, & Woolley, 2013).

Second, the intrinsic view of ambiguity describes situations in which it is a given condition of organizational decision-making processes. For instance, studies on causal ambiguity typically assume that while an organization and its competitors perceive the relationship between their actions and successful performance as ambiguous, they do not problematize the various aspects of ambiguity (Mosakowski, 1997). This is attributable to their limited cognitive capacities and their bounded rationality, which prevent them from predicting cause–effect relationships with certainty. In emergent perspectives on the topic, ambiguity may instead vary in intensity over time (Denis et al., 2011) and type (Cappellaro, Compagni, & Vaara, 2021), depending on the strategic purposes it should fulfil. Similarly, more recent literature on categories shows how ambiguity around an organizational category may be high in the early phases of its development and then fade away once the organization seeks a clear positioning in the market (Granqvist & Ritvala, 2016).

Third, in the intrinsic view, ambiguity originates externally to organizational members when either the environment or the organizational context in which they are embedded sends signals and cues that they interpret as ambiguous. In contrast, the strategic perspectives on strategic ambiguity show how ambiguity originates inside the organization through the interaction of managers and organizational members, for instance during preparatory work for new strategic actions (Sillince, Jarzabkowski, & Shaw, 2012) or organizational change (Sonenshein, 2010). Alternatively, ambiguity develops in the interaction of organizations and their audiences (Guthey & Morsing, 2014), always with organizational members as its prime source. This take on ambiguity can also be found in the latest literature on categories (e.g., Ozcan & Gurses, 2018), in which categories are blurred and made ambiguous by organizations for the purpose of distracting, counteracting, or winning over audiences.

Taken together, our analysis points to two main trajectories in research on ambiguity. We highlight those below and indicate the most promising venues for future research on each.

6.1 Conceptualizing Ambiguity as a Relational Construct

By considering ambiguity across the entire set of studies we have examined in the previous sections, we can draw a trajectory in which it is progressively conceptualized as a relational construct, that is, developing through interaction between different actors both within organizations (e.g., managers and employees) and between organizational members and external audiences. While March conceives of ambiguity as the result of continuous – often conflictual – confrontation between various actors and coalitions within organizations, their diverse goals and interpretations, the subsequent stream of literature examining ambiguity in decision-making has paid less attention to how ambiguity results from interaction within and around organizations. In these studies, ambiguity is portrayed mainly as a property of the information, goals, and contexts or cause–effect relationships characterizing organizational reality. Later on, when the focus in organization studies shifts to organizational talk, discourse, and communication, the social construction of ambiguity and its development in interaction are indeed more readily apparent. In communication studies in particular, as Eisenberg indicated, it is in the relationship between the speaker (his/her intentions when talking) and the receiver (his/her perceptions of what is said) that ambiguity develops. In this view, ambiguity cannot exist without being generated through text that is then perceived as ambiguous.

Despite this shift, only a few studies have fully embraced the relational aspects of ambiguity. Reflecting back on his idea of strategic ambiguity, Eisenberg recently admitted that the relational definition of ambiguity "seemed to make sense at the time but has proven difficult to study" (Eisenberg, 2007: 14). Even among studies in the stream of literature on strategic ambiguity, only a few (Abdallah & Langley, 2014; Cappellaro, Compagni, & Vaara, 2021; Feront & Bertels, 2021; Sonenshein, 2010) are explicit in keeping with this relational conceptualization. For instance, Abdallah and Langley (2014) examine both sides in the relationship developing around ambiguity, that is, those who produce the strategic plans, communicate multiple goals, and create ambiguity through these texts, and those on the receiving end who read and interpret the strategic ambiguity conveyed in the plans. In this sense, it is interesting to note how the authors identify different "forms of consumption" of strategic plans across different organizational audiences and various perceptions of the ambiguity contained in these texts, which lead in turn to a variety of responses. Indeed, these findings show that we have only begun to uncover the nuances of ambiguity-in-interaction.

In what follows, we delineate two avenues of future research that could build upon the idea of ambiguity as a relational construct.

6.1.1 Actorhood and Agency in Ambiguity Management

The first avenue for future research focuses on more effective exploration and theorization of actorhood and agency in ambiguity management. By "ambiguity management" we mean all the processes aimed at creating, responding, exploiting, maintaining, or transforming ambiguity. Future research could focus on which actors within organizations are involved in or take the initiative to manage ambiguity, for what purposes and through what means. Similarly, future research could concentrate on external organizational audiences such as other organizations, politicians, regulators, civil society, the public, or the media –and thereby explain not only the repertoire of responses to organizational ambiguity displayed by them but also how the ambiguity generated by these external social actors impact the reactions of organizations to that ambiguity. For instance, Feront and Bertels (2021) describe how in South Africa the ambiguity included in the framing of socially responsible investment (SRI) by its proponents (mainly regulatory institutions) led not only to a variety of responses (i.e., dissociating, normalizing, and moderating) within financial organizations (asset owners, asset managers, and asset consultants), but also among financial and other organizations in this issue field (e.g., civil society organizations, SRI consultancy firms, and universities). Hence, researchers should therefore focus special attention actorhood that may develop around and be afforded by ambiguity as well as the conditions that generate it.

A good starting point in this respect would be to account for what several authors (Abdallah & Langley, 2014; Feront & Bertels, 2021) describe, that is, polar responses toward ambiguity across organizational members and organizations: on the one hand, responses directed to face and embrace ambiguity and on the other those that reject ambiguity or distance themselves from it. The choice between these two polar responses does not appear to be randomly distributed across individuals or organizations. Hence, aspects such as subject positions, cultural, or social norms may be relevant in informing this choice. As for instance shown by Cappellaro, Compagni, and Vaara (2021), it was only when a certain cultural and social awareness of the problem represented by the mafia emerged that state representatives started to acknowledge the ambiguity surrounding the criminal organization and began to dissipate it through definition and categorization.

Another relevant aspect to understand in this stream of future research is when and toward which audiences organizations decide to make use of ambiguity, that is, the various choices they make in creating ambiguity about their purposes, practices, or conduct, or vice versa in dissipating it. Firms, for instance, may need to use high-level communication toward investors or market analysts who evaluate their viability (Zuckerman, 1999) or employ ambiguous labels toward clients in order to reach a much broader range of people (Chliova, Mair, & Vernis, 2020) – or vice versa (Pontikes, 2012). Hence understanding the selective way in which actorhood is exercised in ambiguity management is a fundamental step toward theorizing ambiguity as a relational construct, given that it shows what relationships organizations or organizational members choose or need to "activate" and how.

Exploring actorhood in ambiguity management would also better illuminate the motivations of actors involved and the strategic or instrumental purposes that drive organizations or individuals in so doing.

While, in fact, the literature (e.g., Jarzabkowski, Sillince, & Shaw, 2010; Sonenshein, 2010) has so far explored some of the purposes, such as promoting organizational change and adaptation, creating cohesion, or mobilizing different viewpoints, less attention has been paid to the use of ambiguity within and around organizations to maintain power positions, exercise control by confusing or immobilizing one's counterparts, and exploit (or sometimes abuse) the "deniability" that ambiguity grants to discourse (Eisenberg, 1984) in order to escape blame, responsibility, or stigmatization. However, instead of merely assuming motivations behind the strategic use of ambiguity, scholars may want to investigate them directly, from the vantage points of the protagonists. Why do managers send ambiguous messages to employees? Are they aware the messages are ambiguous? How intentional is a choice, and how much is it something that managers can simply not avoid given the complexities of organizational life? Answering these questions may enable distinguishing intentions from the results of such actions or provide a better understanding of whether and why actors change or correct strategies based on observing the reactions of those who perceive the ambiguity.

Once again, this would allow more thorough exploration of the relationships that organize around ambiguity, their interplay, and the feedback loops. Are those responding to ambiguity aware of their counterparts' intentions? Does this matter for the way they respond? Some of these questions point to the need to expand and integrate our knowledge about responses to ambiguity beyond the more established cognitive explanations to encompass emotional or value-based judgments that may both complement and modify cognitive responses.

6.1.2 Processes and Means of Ambiguity Management

A second stream of future research could focus on the processes and means through which ambiguity management occurs. First, the view of ambiguity as a relational construct brings to the fore the need to theorize ambiguity management as a process unfolding over time, facilitated by relational mechanisms. Abdallah and Langley (2014) point out that the shift over time that they witnessed – from ambiguity that supports change to ambiguity that stymies an organization – is evident in the various responses of different groups in the organization. In other words, the feedback provided by organizational members over time and the relationships among them transform the perception of ambiguity from generative to constraining. Cappellaro, Compagni, and Vaara (2021) show that maintaining strategic ambiguity is based on the interdependent evolution of the strategies for managing ambiguity enacted by the two sides through interaction. If we are to overcome a view of ambiguity management that is abstracted from time and context and to conceptualize it instead as a social construction relevant for individuals and organizations alike, we need a better understanding of how it works, that is, the mechanisms behind its progression or cyclicality and the transformative effect they may have on the nature of the ambiguity at their core.

Second, it is important to extend our underlying views as to how ambiguity is managed within organizations when dealing with complicated or controversial issues. So far, most studies dealing with ambiguity have focused on the classical discursive and rhetorical means (Jarzabkowski, Sillince, & Shaw, 2010; Sillince, Jarzabkowski, & Shaw, 2012) involving rational argumentation or occasionally emotional appeal. It is only relatively recently that, for instance, the underlying value premises – concealed or not – have received attention in this area (Sorsa & Vaara, 2020).

However, other discursive and rhetorical means also play an important role in dealing with ambiguity. This is especially the case with humor and irony, which are often based on double meaning or play with ambiguity (Hatch & Erhlich, 1993; Sewell & Barker, 2006). Interestingly, humor has lately received some attention in research on paradox as a means for coping with controversial perspectives. For instance, Jarzabkowski and Lê (2017) have elaborated on how humor can be used to surface, bring attention to, and make experiences of paradox communicable. Both the need and the ability to deal with contradictions as specific manifestations of ambiguity are at the heart of their analysis. Digging deeper into such discursive and rhetorical processes would seem to be a fruitful avenue for future research to extend and deepen our understanding of the role of humor in dealing with ambiguity.

More specifically, such analysis can focus on irony. By definition, irony allows a stance that is simultaneously associated with two fundamentally different views that are then contrasted to facilitate dealing with complicated issues (Kwon et al., 2020a, 2020b). In a rare study of the use of irony, Kwon et al. (2020a) showed how it can be applied in four different ways when dealing with controversial issues: "acquiescing" (framing understanding as having no alternative because of environmental constraints), "empowering" (synthesizing a view through broad inputs from different individuals), "channeling" (subsuming other interpretations under a dominant view), and "dismissing" (rejecting alternative interpretations and reinforcing the status quo). In another paper, Kwon et al. (2020b) explain how people may construct specific "ironic personae" in order to deal with complicated matters without losing face, thus illuminating another interesting aspect of how ambiguity may be dealt with at the individual level. Future research could zoom in on the use of such discursive or rhetorical strategies in the creation and maintenance of ambiguity in communication at group and organizational levels.

This approach would not only help in advancing specific conceptualizations of ambiguity, but also in developing a theorization of ambiguity as a phenomenon in its own right. In this direction, future research could expand the variety of methods employed to include the analysis of large corpora of text and images. These efforts could capitalize on recent attempts to systematically capture ambiguous language through computational linguistic methodologies and topic modeling (e.g., McMahan & Evans, 2018) combined with the in-depth approaches typical of discourse and rhetorical analyses.

6.2 The Impact of Ambiguity on Organizations and the Role of Mediatized Society

A second trajectory intersecting the two perspectives deals with the impact of ambiguity on organizations. Traditional studies of ambiguity as an inherent part of decision-making start from a premise that ambiguity causes problems in organizational processes. Thus, empirical work in this stream has primarily emphasized the negative impacts of ambiguity on the organization. Such impacts include delaying the decision-making process, biasing its results, leading actors to make random decisions, or deviating from formal structures in the direction of informal networks. In contrast, discursive perspectives on ambiguity primarily elaborate how ambiguity can be deployed strategically by organizational actors to advance their interests. The positive implications of ambiguity have been traced with respect to favoring particular organizational strategic change processes and managing relationships with external stakeholders, as discussed in depth in Section 5. Boundary conditions apply to such positive impacts, and these include the degree of ambiguity instilled in the process, as well as the stage of the change process in which ambiguity is deployed, with planning phases being more likely to benefit from the strategic use of ambiguity than implementation phases. A core difference between the two perspectives is what drives such organizational impacts, with the former view focusing on the features of a general, indistinct ambiguous context upon which members can exert little agency, and the latter on interaction with specific groups of stakeholders holding competing views. These stakeholders could be internal to organizations, as in the case of employees implementing change initiatives, or external, as in the case of clients or shareholders.

However, it is important to note that the distinction between positive and negative outcomes does not strictly demarcate the two perspectives. For example, both the resource-based view literature on causal complexity and some of March's work position ambiguity as positive. Similarly, the discursive constructions of ambiguity could be harmful, marginalizing, purposefully misleading, or otherwise problematic, depending on the specific actors and their interests, as in the case of the Mafia (Cappellaro, Compagni, & Vaara, 2021). Thus, developing more nuanced understanding of the effects is a major challenge for future research.

While the strategic view on discursively constructed strategic ambiguity focuses on communication as a key determinant of the impact of ambiguity on organizations, it would be important to dig deeper into the new forms and manifestations of communication mediate such effects. Specifically, research on ambiguity has not focused adequate attention on the fundamental role of mediatization in contemporary society and its effects on organizations and organizing. Hence, there is a need to update and extend our theoretical understanding of the consequences and impacts of ambiguity on organizations that operate in increasingly mediatized environments.

In the following, we unpack our arguments on the role of ambiguity in mediatized societies by highlighting three particularly relevant ideas for future research: structural and politicized ambiguity in "post-truth" society, ambiguity in "bullshit" organizational communication, and ambiguity in multimodal strategic communication.

6.2.1 Structural and Politicized Ambiguity in Post-Truth Society and "Bullshit-type" Ambiguity

We are living in a mediatized society where developments in recent decades have revolutionized communication in mass and social media. Among other things this has led to – or at least been part of –increasing polarization in communication to the extent that people have started to use the term "post-truth" society (Knight & Tsoukas, 2019; Parker & Racz, 2020). We have therefore seen how alternative viewpoints and truths have become an essential part of strategic communication. This has also been linked with the creation of "bubbles" of communication where like-minded people can reinforce specific views and interpretations, even apparently distorted or fictitious ones, in their own platforms or spheres.

This multiplicity of truths can be seen as a new structural form of ambiguity that should also be taken seriously in organizational research. It involves both more formal communication strategies used by organizations and more informal communication for example in social media. The point is that many controversial organizational issues, decisions, and actions may become subjects of discussion where ambiguity rather than unanimity about the facts, interpretations, and implications prevails. Moreover, it has become easier for people to raise awareness and target specific organizations or their representatives – for both good and bad. Examples of "good" may be seen in social movements like "MeToo," "Black Lives Matter," or climate change where companies have become part of wider societal struggles. Examples of "bad" may include scapegoating or sabotage based, for instance, on the toxic material of "deep fakes." It would be important to examine how this kind of structural and politicized ambiguity characterizes and affects strategic communication in and around the organizations of both today and tomorrow. This could also involve strategic production of fake news or spreading of conspiracy theories. What are the implications of this type of ambiguity for organizations? What are the potentials and limits for organizations to leverage on such ambiguity and how does its use impact the processes of discursive legitimation or identity construction?

A second feature of mediatized society is the increasing role of the superficial or vacuous in organizational communication. Rather than proposing alternative truths, this type of communication is characterized by "bullshit," that is, a provocative term that aptly captures aspects of communication that are instrumental in promoting specific discourses but meaningless in content. For instance, the philosopher Harry Frankfurt views bullshit as talk that has no concern for the truth (Frankfurt, 2009). This kind of communication can be linked specifically with the business or management jargon that has become widespread, but is often characterized by window-dressing, political correctness, or sheer emptiness in substance – at times more deliberate, at other times more mindless (Spicer, 2017, 2020). This kind of communication can be seen as another new type of ambiguity; in this case, the ambiguity emerges from the juxtaposition of meaningful and meaningless communication. Thus, it would be interesting and important to dig deeper into the role of "bullshit ambiguity" in organizations and focus on its consequences. For example, how does the nature of ambiguity – for example, ambiguity based on multiple meanings vis-à-vis ambiguity based on meaningful and meaningless contents – inform the range of potential organizational strategies in order to influence internal and external stakeholders? What are the consequences for organizational legitimacy, identity or power relations?

6.2.2 Ambiguity in Multimodal Strategic Communication

From another kind of perspective, mediatized society alerts us to the importance of updating our understanding of multimodality in organizational communication and its implications for ambiguity. Communication has been and will always be in some ways multimodal (Kress & Van Leeuwen, 2001). A mode is a "semiotic resource which allow the simultaneous realization of discourses and types of (inter)action" (Kress & Van Leeuwen, 2001: 21); examples of modes are language, images or music. The meaning potential of individual modes is culturally and historically contingent (Jancsary, Höllerer, & Meyer, 2016). In today's mediatized society, the role of different communication modes, especially visual communication, has been accentuated (Höllerer et al., 2019). Consequently, attention should be focused not only on verbal or textual communication, but also on the use of visual and other types of multimodal materials in organizational communication to gain a better understanding of the discursive and rhetorical processes involving strategic ambiguity. We contend that such understanding encompasses two complimentary domains: the relationship between ambiguity and visual communication and that between ambiguity and multimodal communication – where visuals are one mode of communication.

As to the former, there are two key issues for research on ambiguity: can visual communication be more ambiguous than written or verbal communication and what are its implications for organizational processes? By visual communication we refer not only to images, but also to videos, graphs, diagrams, as well as "the way visual composition integrates text, images, color, and typography into new forms of writing that combine words into messages through a visual rather than a linguistic syntax" (Höllerer et al., 2019).The question of the ambiguity in visual communication has been debated in communication studies (Eppler, Mengis, & Bresciani, 2008) and has begun to gain traction in organization studies (Höllerer, Jancsary, & Grafström, 2018; Quattrone, 2017; Quattrone et al., 2021). The ambiguity of visual communication relies on the polysemic character of images (Barthes, 1977), where the image connotations change in accordance with both the context of the image and the characteristics of the viewer (Eppler, Mengis, & Bresciani, 2008: 2). Based on the inherently relational view of ambiguity, some scholars have reflected on the core dimensions of visual ambiguity – that is, the properties of the visual, the people interpreting the visual, and the interaction among people through the visual – and elaborated a taxonomy of visual ambiguity (iconic ambiguity, symbolic ambiguity, indexical ambiguity, background ambiguity, familiarity ambiguity, focus ambiguity, and scope ambiguity) (Eppler, Mengis, & Bresciani, 2008).

The question of the impacts of visual ambiguity on organizations remains unresolved. In support of a positive correlation between visuals and ambiguity, it can be argued that the power of imagery is often linked to the emotional appeal that builds on various elements and their meaning potential. In this way, visual communication tends to be more ambiguous. This is because its appeal, while powerful, may also be vague (as in unclarity) and therefore subject to various interpretations that facilitate connections with multiple audiences and discourses (as in equivocality). Since visuals can mirror, mask, and constitute social reality, such ambiguity can be leveraged strategically (Jancsary, Höllerer, & Meyer, 2016). Hence it would be important to update our understanding of the various discursive and rhetorical strategies generated by managers and organizational members through visuals as well as their complex and ambiguous effects on organizations.

Besides the study of visual communication, it would be important to reflect on the implications for ambiguity of the relationships between the various modes characterizing multimodal discourse. In fact, integration of modes in multimodal texts is gaining attention in organization studies (Boxenbaum et al., 2018; Höllerer, Daudigeos, & Jancsary, 2017). For the most part, scholars have attempted to identify principles for positive integration (Van Leeuwen, 2005); these include "genre, rhythm, visual composition, conjunction, and dialogue structure" (Höllerer et al., 2019). However, as each mode has its own way of constructing and transforming reality (Meyer et al., 2013), it would be important to study ambiguous multimodal communication in the strategic use of multiple modes, also in apparent contrast one with the other, and its implication for organizations. Future research could thus employ multimodal discourse analysis techniques to disentangle such relationships.

7 Conclusion

In this Element, we have described how ambiguity has been able to stimulate the interest of organizational theorists for over sixty years. We have shown how starting from the seminal work of James March a very rich tradition has evolved through examination of the roles and impacts of ambiguity on organizational decision-making processes and how, with the discursive turn in organization studies, a further widening of the conceptualization of ambiguity and its relevance for organizations has occurred. This has opened up new research avenues aimed at understanding the strategic use of ambiguity in discourse and communication within and around organizations. It is also engendering interest in improving theorization regarding the purpose for which ambiguity is used, the means and processes through which organizations manage it, and the impact thereof. Overall, these trajectories are forcing scholars to bring the social role of organizations front and center and account for how organizations contribute and respond to the ambiguity associated with controversial issues of social and political relevance and to mediatization of our societies.

In this Element, we have also highlighted how ambiguity has crossed paths over time with a number of neighboring concepts such as uncertainty, equivocality, polyphony, and, more recently, paradox, thereby allowing fruitful, though sometimes confusing, cross-fertilizations among theoretical lenses, disciplines, and worlds of research. In other words, the ambiguity of ambiguity has allowed scholars to make substantial advances in organization theory, stimulated constant and fervid recasting thereof, and spurred fundamental reflections on our "organized" lives.

As the introductory quote by March testifies, ambiguity can deeply touch and stimulate individuals and organizations at very many levels. It affects cognition, emotions, relations; it works on values, identity, and experience. Although it may be disturbing and destabilizing, its impact can also be magical. It must therefore be seen as a key part of organization theory and practice – and a topic that deserves special attention now and in the future.

References

Abdallah, C. and A. Langley (2014). The double edge of ambiguity in strategic planning. *Journal of Management Studies* **51**(2): 235–264.

Adler, P. S. (1995). Interdepartmental interdependence and coordination: The case of the design/manufacturing interface. *Organization Science* **6**(2): 147–167.

Aggerholm, H. K., B. Asmuß and C. Thomsen (2012). The role of recontextualization in the multivocal, ambiguous process of strategizing. *Journal of Management Inquiry* **21**(4): 413–428.

Allen, L. E. (1958). Toward more clarity in business communications by modern logical methods. *Management Science* **5**(1): 121–135.

Altomonte, G. (2020). Exploiting ambiguity: A moral polysemy approach to variation in economic practices. *American Sociological Review* **85**(1): 76–105.

Alvesson, M. (1993). Organizations as rhetoric: Knowledge-intensive firms and the struggle with ambiguity. *Journal of Management Studies* **30**(6): 997–1015.

Alvesson, M. (2001). Knowledge work: Ambiguity, image and identity. *Human Relations* **54**(7): 863–886.

Alvesson, M. and S. Sveningsson (2003). Good visions, bad micro-management and ugly ambiguity: Contradictions of (non-) leadership in a knowledge-intensive organization. *Organization Studies* **24**(6): 961–988.

Ambrosini, V. and C. Bowman (2010). The impact of causal ambiguity on competitive advantage and rent appropriation. *British Journal of Management* **21**(4): 939–953.

Augustine, G., S. Soderstrom, D. Milner and K. Weber (2019). Constructing a distant future: Imaginaries in geoengineering. *Academy of Management Journal* **62**(6): 1930–1960.

Bakhtin, M. (1984). *Problems of Dostoevsky's Poetics*. Minneapolis, University of Minnesota Press.

Bakhtin, M. M. (1982). *The dialogic imagination: Four essays*. Austin, University of Texas Press.

Barney, J. (1991). Firm resources and sustained competitive advantage. *Journal of Management* **17**(1): 99–120.

Bartel, C. A. and B. M. Wiesenfeld (2013). The social negotiation of group prototype ambiguity in dynamic organizational contexts. *Academy of Management Review* **38**(4): 503–524.

Barthes, R. (1977). *Image Music Text*. Essays selected and translated by S. Heath. London: Fontana.

Beckman, C. M. (2021). Alternatives and complements to rationality. In C.M. Beckman (Ed.), *Carnegie goes to California: Advancing and celebrating the work of James G. March* (pp. 3–18). Bingley, Emerald.

Belova, O., I. King and M. Sliwa (2008). Introduction: Polyphony and organization studies: Mikhail Bakhtin and beyond. *Organization Studies* **29**(4): 493–500.

Benders, J. and K. Van Veen (2001). What's in a fashion? Interpretative viability and management fashions. *Organization* **8**(1): 33–53.

Boghossian, J. and R. J. David (2021). Under the umbrella: Goal-derived category construction and product category nesting. *Administrative Science Quarterly*. **66**(4), 1084–1129. https://doi.org/10.1177/00018392211012376.

Boje, D. M. (2008). *Storytelling organizations*. London, Sage.

Boulongne, R. and R. Durand (2021). Evaluating ambiguous offerings. *Organization Science* **32**(2): 257–272.

Boxenbaum, E., C. Jones, R. E. Meyer and S. Svejenova (2018). Towards an articulation of the material and visual turn in organization studies. *Organization Studies* **39**(5–6), 597–616. https://doi.org/10.1177/01708406 18772611.

Boyd, B. K., D. D. Bergh and D. J. Ketchen Jr (2010). Reconsidering the reputation – Performance relationship: A resource-based view. *Journal of Management* **36**(3): 588–609.

Bozeman, B. and G. Kingsley (1998). Risk culture in public and private organizations. *Public Administration Review* **58**(2): 109–118.

Bridwell-Mitchell, E. N. (2016). Collaborative institutional agency: How peer learning in communities of practice enables and inhibits micro-institutional change. *Organization Studies* **37**(2): 161–192.

Bruneau, T. J. (1973). Communicative silences: Forms and functions. *Journal of Communication* **23**(1): 17–46.

Burns, T. and G. M. Stalker (1961). *The management of innovation*. London, Tavistock.

Cappelen, S. M. and J. Strandgaard Pedersen (2021). Inventing culinary heritage through strategic historical ambiguity. *Organization Studies* **42**(2): 223–243.

Cappellaro, G., A. Compagni and E. Vaara (2021). Maintaining strategic ambiguity for protection: Struggles over opacity, equivocality, and absurdity around the Sicilian Mafia. *Academy of Management Journal* **64**(1): 1–37.

Carson, S. J., A. Madhok and T. Wu (2006). Uncertainty, opportunism, and governance: The effects of volatility and ambiguity on formal and relational contracting. *Academy of Management Journal* **49**(5): 1058–1077.

Chliova, M., J. Mair and A. Vernis (2020). Persistent category ambiguity: The case of social entrepreneurship. *Organization Studies* **41**(7): 1019–1042.

Chun, Y. H. and H. G. Rainey (2005). Goal ambiguity and organizational performance in US federal agencies. *Journal of Public Administration Research and Theory* **15**(4): 529–557.

Coff, R. and D. Kryscynski (2011). Invited editorial: Drilling for micro-foundations of human capital-based competitive advantages. *Journal of Management* **37**(5): 1429–1443.

Coff, R. W. (1999). When competitive advantage doesn't lead to performance: The resource-based view and stakeholder bargaining power. *Organization Science* **10**(2): 119–133.

Cohen, M. D. and J. G. March (1974). *Leadership and ambiguity: The American college president.* New York, McGraw-Hill.

Cohen, M. D., J. G. March and J. P. Olsen (1972). A garbage can model of organizational choice. *Administrative Science Quarterly* **17**(1): 1–25.

Contractor, N. S. and M. C. Ehrlich (1993). Strategic ambiguity in the birth of a loosely coupled organization: The case of a \$50-million experiment. *Management Communication Quarterly* **6**(3): 251–281.

Coopey, J., O. Keegan and N. Emler (1998). Managers' innovations and the structuration of organizations. *Journal of Management Studies* **35**(3): 263–284.

Cording, M., P. Christmann and D. R. King (2008). Reducing causal ambiguity in acquisition integration: Intermediate goals as mediators of integration decisions and acquisition performance. *Academy of Management Journal* **51**(4): 744–767.

Cornelissen, J. P., S. Mantere and E. Vaara (2014). The contraction of meaning: The combined effect of communication, emotions, and materiality on sense-making in the Stockwell shooting. *Journal of Management Studies* **51**(5): 699–736.

Cyert, R. M. and J. G. March (1963). *A behavioral theory of the firm.* Englewood Cliffs, Prentice Hall.

Daft, R. L. and R. H. Lengel (1986). Organizational information require-ments, media richness and structural design. *Management Science* **32**(5): 554–571.

Daft, R. L. and N. B. Macintosh (1981). A tentative exploration into the amount and equivocality of information processing in organizational work units. *Administrative Science Quarterly*: **26**(2): 207–224.

Daft, R. L. and K. E. Weick (1984). Toward a model of organizations as interpretation systems. *Academy of Management Review* **9**(2): 284–295.

Dandridge, T. C., I. Mitroff and W. F. Joyce (1980). Organizational symbolism: A topic to expand organizational analysis. *Academy of Management Review* **5**(1): 77–82.

Davenport, S. and S. Leitch (2005). Circuits of power in practice: Strategic ambiguity as delegation of authority. *Organization Studies* **26**(11): 1603–1623.

Davis, R. S. and E. C. Stazyk (2015). Developing and testing a new goal taxonomy: Accounting for the complexity of ambiguity and political support. *Journal of Public Administration Research and Theory* **25**(3): 751–775.

Denis, J.-L., G. Dompierre, A. Langley and L. Rouleau (2011). Escalating indecision: Between reification and strategic ambiguity. *Organization Science* **22**(1): 225–244.

Denis, J.-L., A. Langley and L. Cazale (1996). Leadership and strategic change under ambiguity. *Organization Studies* **17**(4): 673–699.

Donnelly, R. (2011). The ambiguities and tensions in creating and capturing value: Views from HRM consultants in a leading consultancy firm. *Human Resource Management* **50**(3): 425–440.

Duhaime, I. M. and C. R. Schwenk (1985). Conjectures on cognitive simplification in acquisition and divestment decision making. *Academy of Management Review* **10**(2): 287–295.

Durand, R., and Boulongne, R. (2017). Advancing research on categories for institutional approaches of organizations. In R. Greenwood, C. Oliver, T. B. Lawrence, and R. E. Meyer (Eds.), *The SAGE Handbook of Organizational Institutionalism, 2nd ed*. London, Sage.

Edelman, M. (1977). *Political language: Words that succeed and policies that fail*. New York, Academic Press.

Eisenberg, E. M. (1984). Ambiguity as strategy in organizational communication. *Communication Monographs* **51**(3): 227–242.

Eisenberg, E. M. (2007). *Strategic ambiguities: Essays on communication, organization, and identity*. London, Sage.

Eisenberg, E. M., H. L. Goodall Jr and A. Trethewey (2013). *Organizational communication: Balancing creativity and constraint*. Macmillan Higher Education, London, UK.

Eisenberg, E. M. and P. Riley (1988). Organizational symbols and sense-making. *Handbook of Organizational Communication*, 6th ed. (pp. 31–150) **131**. Boston, Bedford/St. Martin's.

Eisenberg, E. M. and M. G. Witten (1987). Reconsidering openness in organizational communication. *Academy of Management Review* **12**(3): 418–426.

Eppler, M. J., J. Mengis and S. Bresciani (2008). *Seven types of visual ambiguity: On the merits and risks of multiple interpretations of collaborative visualizations*. 2008 12th International Conference Information Visualisation, IEEE.

Etter, M., E. Colleoni, L. Illia, K. Meggiorin and A. D'Eugenio (2018). Measuring organizational legitimacy in social media: Assessing citizens' judgments with sentiment analysis. *Business & Society* **57**(1): 60–97.

Faircloth, A. W. and D. N. Ricchiute (1981). Ambiguity intolerance and financial reporting alternatives. *Accounting, Organizations and Society* **6**(1): 53–67.

Fairclough, N. (2001). *Language and power*. Harlow, Pearson Education.

Fairhurst, G. T., W. K. Smith, S. G. Banghart et al. (2016). Diverging and converging: Integrative insights on a paradox meta-perspective. *Academy of Management Annals* **10**(1): 173–182.

Farjoun, M. (2016). Contradictions, dialectics, and paradoxes. In A. Langley and H. Tsoukas (Eds.), *The Sage handbook of process organization studies* (pp. 87–109). London, Sage.

Feldman, M. (1991). The meanings of ambiguity: Learning from stories and metaphors. In P. Frost, L. Moore, M. Reis Louis, C. Lundberg and J. Martin (Eds.), *Reframing organizational culture* (pp. 145–156). Newbury Park, Sage.

Feldman, M. P., S. Ozcan and T. Reichstein (2019). Falling not far from the tree: Entrepreneurs and organizational heritage. *Organization Science* **30**(2): 337–360.

Feldman, M. S. (1989). *Order without design: Information production and policy making*. Stanford, Stanford University Press.

Feront, C. and S. Bertels (2021). The impact of frame ambiguity on field-level change. *Organization Studies* **42**(7): 1135–1165.

Fleischer, A. (2009). Ambiguity and the equity of rating systems: United States brokerage firms, 1995–2000. *Administrative Science Quarterly* **54**(4): 555–574.

Forbes, D. P. (2007). Reconsidering the strategic implications of decision comprehensiveness. *Academy of Management Review* **32**(2): 361–376.

Frankfurt, H. G. (2009). *On bullshit*. Princeton, Princeton University Press.

Garud, R. and A. H. Van de Ven (1992). An empirical evaluation of the internal corporate venturing process. *Strategic Management Journal* **13**(S1): 93–109.

Gavetti, G. and M. Warglien (2015). A model of collective interpretation. *Organization Science* **26**(5): 1263–1283.

Gioia, D. A., R. Nag and K. G. Corley (2012). Visionary ambiguity and strategic change: The virtue of vagueness in launching major organizational change. *Journal of Management Inquiry* **21**(4): 364–375.

Giroux, H. (2006). "It was such a handy term": Management fashions and pragmatic ambiguity. *Journal of Management Studies* **43**(6): 1227–1260.

Glazer, A. (1990). The strategy of candidate ambiguity. *American Political Science Review* **84**(1): 237–241.

Glozer, S., R. Caruana and S. A. Hibbert (2019). The never-ending story: Discursive legitimation in social media dialogue. *Organization Studies* **40**(5): 625–650.

Gonzalez-Mulé, E., S. H. Courtright, D. DeGeest, J.-Y. Seong and D.-S. Hong (2016). Channeled autonomy: The joint effects of autonomy and feedback on team performance through organizational goal clarity. *Journal of Management* **42**(7): 2018–2033.

Gottschalg, O. and M. Zollo (2007). Interest alignment and competitive advantage. *Academy of Management Review* **32**(2): 418–437.

Granqvist, N., S. Grodal and J. L. Woolley (2013). Hedging your bets: Explaining executives' market labeling strategies in nanotechnology. *Organization Science* **24**(2): 395–413.

Granqvist, N. and T. Ritvala (2016). Beyond prototypes: Drivers of market categorization in functional foods and nanotechnology. *Journal of Management Studies* **53**(2): 210–237.

Guthey, E. and M. Morsing (2014). CSR and the mediated emergence of strategic ambiguity. *Journal of Business Ethics* **120**(4): 555–569.

Haas, M. R. (2006). Knowledge gathering, team capabilities, and project performance in challenging work environments. *Management Science* **52**(8): 1170–1184.

Hahn, T., L. Preuss, J. Pinkse and F. Figge (2014). Cognitive frames in corporate sustainability: Managerial sensemaking with paradoxical and business case frames. *Academy of Management Review* **39**(4): 463–487.

Hatch, M. J. and S. B. Erhlich (1993). Spontaneous humour as an indicator of paradox and ambiguity in organizations. *Organization Studies* **14**(4): 505–526.

Hazen, M. A. (1993). Towards polyphonic organization. *Journal of Organizational Change Management* **6**(5): 15–26.

Heide, J. B. and A. S. Miner (1992). The shadow of the future: Effects of anticipated interaction and frequency of contact on buyer-seller cooperation. *Academy of Management Journal* **35**(2): 265–291.

Hennestad, B. W. (1990). The symbolic impact of double bind leadership: Double bind and the dynamics of organizational culture. *Journal of Management Studies* **27**(3): 265–280.

Höllerer, M. A., T. Daudigeos and D. Jancsary (2017). *Multimodality, meaning, and institutions*. Bingley, Emerald.

Höllerer, M. A., D. Jancsary and M. Grafström (2018). "A picture is worth a thousand words": Multimodal sensemaking of the global financial crisis. *Organization Studies* **39**(5–6): 617–644.

Höllerer, M. A., T. van Leeuwen, D. Jancsary et al. (2019). *Visual and multimodal research in organization and management studies*. Milton Park, Routledge.

Hsieh, C.-C., Z. Ma and K. E. Novoselov (2018). Accounting conservatism, business strategy, and ambiguity. *Accounting, Organizations and Society* **30**: 1e15.

Hubbard, T. D., T. G. Pollock, M. D. Pfarrer and V. P. Rindova (2018). Safe bets or hot hands? How status and celebrity influence strategic alliance formations by newly public firms. *Academy of Management Journal* **61**(5): 1976–1999.

Inkpen, A. C. (2008). Knowledge transfer and international joint ventures: The case of NUMMI and General Motors. *Strategic Management Journal* **29**(4): 447–453.

Jacquart, P. and J. Antonakis (2015). When does charisma matter for top-level leaders? Effect of attributional ambiguity. *Academy of Management Journal* **58**(4): 1051–1074.

Jalonen, K., H. Schildt and E. Vaara (2018). Strategic concepts as micro-level tools in strategic sensemaking. *Strategic Management Journal* **39**(5): 2794–2826.

Jancsary, D., M. A. Höllerer and R. E. Meyer (2016). Critical analysis of visual and multimodal texts. In R. Wodak and M. Meyer (Eds.), *Methods of critical discourse studies*, 3rd ed. (pp. 180–204). London, Sage.

Jarzabkowski, P., J. A. Sillince and D. Shaw (2010). Strategic ambiguity as a rhetorical resource for enabling multiple interests. *Human Relations* **63**(2): 219–248.

Jarzabkowski, P. A. and J. K. Lê (2017). We have to do this and that? You must be joking: Constructing and responding to paradox through humor. *Organization Studies* **38**(3–4): 433–462.

Jones, G. R. (1987). Organization-client transactions and organizational governance structures. *Academy of Management Journal* **30**(2): 197–218.

Joseph, J. and V. Gaba (2015). The fog of feedback: Ambiguity and firm responses to multiple aspiration levels. *Strategic Management Journal* **36**(13): 1960–1978.

Jung, C. S. (2013). Navigating a rough terrain of public management: Examining the relationship between organizational size and effectiveness. *Journal of Public Administration Research and Theory* **23**(3): 663–686.

Jung, C. S. (2014a). Extending the theory of goal ambiguity to programs: Examining the relationship between goal ambiguity and performance. *Public Administration Review* **74**(2): 205–219.

Jung, C. S. (2014b). Organizational goal ambiguity and job satisfaction in the public sector. *Journal of Public Administration Research and Theory* **24**(4): 955–981.

Jung, C. S. (2014c). Why are goals important in the public sector? Exploring the benefits of goal clarity for reducing turnover intention. *Journal of Public Administration Research and Theory* **24**(1): 209–234.

Kelemen, M. (2000). Too much or too little ambiguity: The language of total quality management. *Journal of Management Studies* **37**(4): 483–498.

King, A. W. (2007). Disentangling interfirm and intrafirm causal ambiguity: A conceptual model of causal ambiguity and sustainable competitive advantage. *Academy of Management Review* **32**(1): 156–178.

King, A. W. and A. L. Ranft (2001). Capturing knowledge and knowing through improvisation: What managers can learn from the thoracic surgery board certification process. *Journal of Management* **27**(3): 255–277.

King, A. W. and C. P. Zeithaml (2001). Competencies and firm performance: Examining the causal ambiguity paradox. *Strategic Management Journal* **22**(1): 75–99.

Klein, R. (1982). Performance, evaluation and the NHS: A case study in conceptual perplexity and organizational complexity. *Public Administration* **60**(4): 385–407.

Knight, E. and H. Tsoukas (2019). When fiction trumps truth: What "post-truth" and "alternative facts" mean for management studies. *Organization Studies* **40**(2): 183–197.

Konlechner, S. and V. Ambrosini (2019). Issues and trends in causal ambiguity research: A review and assessment. *Journal of Management* **45**(6): 2352–2386.

Kress, G. and T. Van Leeuwen (2001). *Multimodal discourse: The modes and media of contemporary communication*. London, Arnold.

Kwon, W., I. Clarke, E. Vaara, R. Mackay and R. Wodak (2020a). Using verbal irony to move on with controversial issues. *Organization Science* **31**(4): 865–886.

Kwon, W., R. Mackay, I. Clarke, R. Wodak and E. Vaara (2020b). Testing, stretching, and aligning: Using "ironic personae" to make sense of complicated issues. *Journal of Pragmatics* **166**: 44–58.

Kydd, C. T. (1989). Understanding the information content in MIS management tools. *Mis Quarterly* **13**(3): 277–290.

Lakshman, C. (2011). Postacquisition cultural integration in mergers & acquisitions: A knowledge-based approach. *Human Resource Management* **50**(5): 605–623.

Lee, J. W., H. G. Rainey and Y. H. Chun (2009). Of politics and purpose: Political salience and goal ambiguity of US federal agencies. *Public Administration* **87**(3): 457–484.

Lee, W. E. and A. M. Hageman (2018). Talk the talk or walk the walk? An examination of sustainability accounting implementation. *Journal of Business Ethics* **152**(3): 725–739.

Lei, D., M. A. Hitt and R. Bettis (1996). Dynamic core competences through meta-learning and strategic context. *Journal of Management* **22**(4): 549–569.

Letiche, H. (2010). Polyphony and its other. *Organization Studies* **31**(3): 261–277.

Leitch, S. and S. Davenport (2002). Strategic ambiguity in communicating public sector change. *Journal of Communication Management* **7**(2): 129–139.

Leitch, S. and S. Davenport (2007). Strategic ambiguity as a discourse practice: The role of keywords in the discourse on "sustainable" biotechnology. *Discourse Studies* **9**(1): 43–61.

Levinthal, D. and J. G. March (1981). A model of adaptive organizational search. *Journal of Economic Behavior & Organization* **2**(4): 307–333.

Levinthal, D. A. and C. Rerup (2021). The plural of goal: Learning in a world of ambiguity. *Organization Science* **32**(3): 527–543.

Lewis, M. W. (2000). Exploring paradox: Toward a more comprehensive guide. *Academy of Management Review* **25**(4): 760–776.

Lingo, E. L. and S. O'Mahony (2010). Nexus work: Brokerage on creative projects. *Administrative Science Quarterly* **55**(1): 47–81.

Lippman, S. A. and R. P. Rumelt (1982). Uncertain imitability: An analysis of interfirm differences in efficiency under competition. *The Bell Journal of Economics* **13**(2): 418–438.

Litrico, J.-B. and R. J. David (2017). The evolution of issue interpretation within organizational fields: Actor positions, framing trajectories, and field settlement. *Academy of Management Journal* **60**(3): 986–1015.

Lockett, A. and S. Thompson (2001). The resource-based view and economics. *Journal of Management* **27**(6): 723–754.

Luscher, L. S., M. Lewis and A. Ingram (2006). The social construction of organizational change paradoxes. *Journal of Organizational Change Management* **19**(4): 491–502.

Maitlis, S. and M. Christianson (2014). Sensemaking in organizations: Taking stock and moving forward. *Academy of Management Annals* **8**(1): 57–125.

Maitlis, S. and H. Ozcelik (2004). Toxic decision processes: A study of emotion and organizational decision making. *Organization Science* **15**(4): 375–393.

March, J., Ed. (1965). *Handbook of organizations*. Chicago, Rand McNally.

March, J. G. (1958). A behavioral theory of decision making. *Personnel Administration* **21**(3): 8–10.

March, J. G. (1962). The business firm as a political coalition. *The Journal of Politics* **24**(4): 662–678.

March, J. G. (1978). Bounded rationality, ambiguity, and the engineering of choice. *The Bell Journal of Economics* **9**(2): 587–608.

March, J. G. (1994). *Primer on decision making: How decisions happen.* Manhattan, Simon and Schuster.

March, J. G. (2010). *The ambiguities of experience.* Cornell University Press.

March, J. G. and J. P. Olsen (1976). *Ambiguity and choice in organizations.* Ithaca, Bergen, Univeritetsforlaget.

March, J. G. and H. A. Simon (1958). *Organizations.* New York, Wiley.

Markham, A. (1996). Designing discourse: A critical analysis of strategic ambiguity and workplace control. *Management Communication Quarterly* **9**(4): 389–421.

McEvily, S. K., S. Das and K. McCabe (2000). Avoiding competence substitution through knowledge sharing. *Academy of Management Review* **25**(2): 294–311.

McMahan, P. and J. Evans (2018). Ambiguity and engagement. *American Journal of Sociology* **124**(3): 860–912.

Meszaros, J. R. (1999). Preventive choices: Organizations' heuristics, decision processes and catastrophic risks. *Journal of Management Studies* **36**(7): 977–998.

Meyer, R. E. and M. A. Höllerer (2016). Laying a smoke screen: Ambiguity and neutralization as strategic responses to intra-institutional complexity. *Strategic Organization* **14**(4): 373–406.

Meyer, R. E., M. A. Höllerer, D. Jancsary and T. Van Leeuwen (2013). The visual dimension in organizing, organization, and organization research: Core ideas, current developments, and promising avenues. *Academy of Management Annals* **7**(1): 489–555.

Mosakowski, E. (1997). Strategy making under causal ambiguity: Conceptual issues and empirical evidence. *Organization Science* **8**(4): 414–442.

Moussavi, F. and D. A. Evans (1993). Emergence of organizational attributions: The role of a shared cognitive schema. *Journal of Management* **19**(1): 79–95.

Moynihan, D. P. (2006). What do we talk about when we talk about performance? Dialogue theory and performance budgeting. *Journal of Public Administration Research and Theory* **16**(2): 151–168.

Munro, R. (1995). Managing by ambiguity: An archaeology of the social in the absence of management accounting. *Critical Perspectives on Accounting* **6**(5): 433–482.

Navis, C. and M. A. Glynn (2011). Legitimate distinctiveness and the entrepreneurial identity: Influence on investor judgments of new venture plausibility. *Academy of Management Review* **36**(3): 479–499.

Nicolai, A. T. and J. M. Dautwiz (2010). Fuzziness in action: What consequences has the linguistic ambiguity of the core competence concept for organizational usage? *British Journal of Management* **21**(4): 874–888.

Noval, L. J. and M. Hernandez (2019). The unwitting accomplice: How organizations enable motivated reasoning and self-serving behavior. *Journal of Business Ethics* **157**(3): 699–713.

Ouchi, W. G. (1980). Markets, bureaucracies, and clans. *Administrative Science Quarterly* **25**(1): 129–141.

Ozcan, P. and K. Gurses (2018). Playing cat and mouse: Contests over regulatory categorization of dietary supplements in the United States. *Academy of Management Journal* **61**(5): 1789–1820.

Packard, M. D., B. B. Clark and P. G. Klein (2017). Uncertainty types and transitions in the entrepreneurial process. *Organization Science* **28**(5): 840–856.

Padgett, J. F. and C. K. Ansell (1993). Robust action and the rise of the Medici, 1400–1434. *American Journal of Sociology* **98**(6): 1259–1319.

Page, B. I. (1976). The theory of political ambiguity. *American Political Science Review* **70**(3): 742–752.

Parker, S. and M. Racz (2020). Affective and effective truths: Rhetoric, normativity and critical management studies. *Organization* **27**(3): 454–465.

Paul, J. and C. A. Strbiak (1997). The ethics of strategic ambiguity. *The Journal of Business Communication* **34**(2): 149–159.

Pescosolido, A. T. (2002). Emergent leaders as managers of group emotion. *The Leadership Quarterly* **13**(5): 583–599.

Petkova, A. P., A. Wadhwa, X. Yao and S. Jain (2014). Reputation and decision making under ambiguity: A study of US venture capital firms' investments in the emerging clean energy sector. *Academy of Management Journal* **57**(2): 422–448.

Pfeffer, J. (1981). Management as symbolic action: The creation and maintenance of organizational paradigm. *Research in Organizational Behavior* **3**: 1–52.

Phillips, N. and C. Oswick (2012). Organizational discourse: Domains, debates, and directions. *Academy of Management Annals* **6**(1): 435–481.

Pich, M. T., C. H. Loch and A. D. Meyer (2002). On uncertainty, ambiguity, and complexity in project management. *Management Science* **48**(8): 1008–1023.

Pinder, C. C. and K. P. Harlos (2001). Employee silence: Quiescence and acquiescence as responses to perceived injustice. In *Research in personnel and human resources management* (pp. 331–369). Bingley, Emerald Group.

Pontikes, E. G. (2012). Two sides of the same coin: How ambiguous classification affects multiple audiences' evaluations. *Administrative Science Quarterly* **57**(1): 81–118.

Powell, T. C., D. Lovallo and C. Caringal (2006). Causal ambiguity, management perception, and firm performance. *Academy of Management Review* **31**(1): 175–196.

Purcell, J. and A. Gray (1986). Corporate personnel departments and the management of industrial relations: Two case studies in ambiguity. *Journal of Management Studies* **23**(2): 205–223.

Putnam, L. and M. E. Pacanowsky (1983). *Communication and organizations: An interpretive approach.* London, Sage.

Putnam, L. L. (1986). Contradictions and paradoxes in organizations. In L. Thayer (Ed.), *Organization-communication: Emerging perspectives* (pp. 151–167). Norwood, Ablex.

Putnam, L. L., G. T. Fairhurst and S. Banghart (2016). Contradictions, dialectics, and paradoxes in organizations: A constitutive approach. *Academy of Management Annals* **10**(1): 65–171.

Quattrone, P. (2017). Embracing ambiguity in management controls and decision-making processes: On how to design data visualisations to prompt wise judgement. *Accounting and Business Research* **47**(5): 588–612.

Quattrone, P., M. Ronzani, D. Jancsary and M. A. Höllerer (2021). Beyond the visible, the material and the performative: Shifting perspectives on the visual in organization studies. *Organization Studies* **42**(8): 1197–1218.

Rainey, H. G. and B. Bozeman (2000). Comparing public and private organizations: Empirical research and the power of the a priori. *Journal of Public Administration Research and Theory* **10**(2): 447–470.

Rainey, H. G. and C. S. Jung (2015). A conceptual framework for analysis of goal ambiguity in public organizations. *Journal of Public Administration Research and Theory* **25**(1): 71–99.

Rajagopalan, N. and S. Finkelstein (1992). Effects of strategic orientation and environmental change on senior management reward systems. *Strategic Management Journal* **13**(S1): 127–141.

Ramsay, J. (2004). Trope control: The costs and benefits of metaphor unreliability in the description of empirical phenomena. *British Journal of Management* **15**(2): 143–155.

Reed, R. and R. J. DeFillippi (1990). Causal ambiguity, barriers to imitation, and sustainable competitive advantage. *Academy of Management Review* **15**(1): 88–102.

Richards, I. A. (1936). *The philosophy of rhetoric.* Oxford, Clarendon Press.

Rindova, V., W. J. Ferrier and R. Wiltbank (2010). Value from gestalt: How sequences of competitive actions create advantage for firms in nascent markets. *Strategic Management Journal* **31**(13): 1474–1497.

Ring, P. S. and J. L. Perry (1985). Strategic management in public and private organizations: Implications of distinctive contexts and constraints. *Academy of Management Review* **10**(2): 276–286.

Robertson, M. and J. Swan (2003). "Control – What control?" Culture and ambiguity within a knowledge intensive firm. *Journal of Management Studies* **40**(4): 831–858.

Ruefli, T. and J. Sarrazin (1981). Strategic control of corporate development under ambiguous circumstances. *Management Science* **27**(10): 1158–1170.

Ryall, M. D. (2009). Causal ambiguity, complexity, and capability-based advantage. *Management Science* **55**(3): 389–403.

Sarasvathy, S. D., N. Dew, S. Read and R. Wiltbank (2008). Designing organizations that design environments: Lessons from entrepreneurial expertise. *Organization Studies* **29**(3): 331–350.

Scandelius, C. and G. Cohen (2016). Achieving collaboration with diverse stakeholders – The role of strategic ambiguity in CSR communication. *Journal of Business Research* **69**(9): 3487–3499.

Schad, J., M. W. Lewis, S. Raisch and W. K. Smith (2016). Paradox research in management science: Looking back to move forward. *Academy of Management Annals* **10**(1): 5–64.

Schramm, C. J. (1975). Thompson's assessment of organizations: Universities and the AAUP salary grades. *Administrative Science Quarterly* **20**(1): 87–96.

Schwenk, C. R. (1988). Effects of devil's advocacy on escalating commitment. *Human Relations* **41**(10): 769–782.

Sellnow, T. L. and R. R. Ulmer (1995). Ambiguous argument as advocacy in organizational crisis communication. *Argumentation and Advocacy* **31**(3): 138–150.

Sewell, G. and J. R. Barker (2006). Coercion versus care: Using irony to make sense of organizational surveillance. *Academy of Management Review* **31**(4): 934–961.

Sgourev, S. V. (2013). How Paris gave rise to Cubism (and Picasso): Ambiguity and fragmentation in radical innovation. *Organization Science* **24**(6): 1601–1617.

Shepsle, K. A. (1972). The strategy of ambiguity: Uncertainty and electoral competition. *American Political Science Review* **66**(2): 555–568.

Shon, J., G. A. Porumbescu and R. K. Christensen (2020). Can budget ambiguity crowd out intrinsic motivation? Longitudinal evidence from federal executive departments. *Public Administration* **98**(1): 194–209.

Sillince, J., P. Jarzabkowski and D. Shaw (2012). Shaping strategic action through the rhetorical construction and exploitation of ambiguity. *Organization Science* **23**(3): 630–650.

Simon, H. A. (1947). *Administrative behavior: A study of decision-making processes in administrative organization*. New York, Macmillan.

Simon, H. A. (1959). Theories of decision making in economics and behavioral science. *American Economic Review* **49**: 253–283.

Smith, W. K. and M. W. Lewis (2011). Toward a theory of paradox: A dynamic equilibrium model of organizing. *Academy of Management Review* **36**(2): 381–403.

Sonenshein, S. (2010). We're changing – Or are we? Untangling the role of progressive, regressive, and stability narratives during strategic change implementation. *Academy of Management Journal* **53**(3): 477–512.

Sorensen, R. (2003). *A brief history of the paradox: Philosophy and the labyrinths of the mind*. Oxford, Oxford University Press.

Sorsa, V. and E. Vaara (2020). How can pluralistic organizations proceed with strategic change? A processual account of rhetorical contestation, convergence, and partial agreement in a Nordic city organization. *Organization Science* **31**(4): 839–864.

Spee, P. and P. Jarzabkowski (2017). Agreeing on what? Creating joint accounts of strategic change. *Organization Science* **28**(1): 152–176.

Spicer, A. (2017). *Business bullshit*. London, Routledge.

Spicer, A. (2020). Playing the bullshit game: How empty and misleading communication takes over organizations. *Organization Theory* **1**(2): 1–26. https://doi.org/10.1177/2631787720929704.

Srivastava, S. B. (2015). Intraorganizational network dynamics in times of ambiguity. *Organization Science* **26**(5): 1365–1380.

Stazyk, E. C. and H. T. Goerdel (2011). The benefits of bureaucracy: Public managers' perceptions of political support, goal ambiguity, and organizational effectiveness. *Journal of Public Administration Research and Theory* **21**(4): 645–672.

Stone, M. M. and C. G. Brush (1996). Planning in ambiguous contexts: The dilemma of meeting needs for commitment and demands for legitimacy. *Strategic Management Journal* **17**(8): 633–652.

Sullivan, P. and J. McCarthy (2008). Managing the polyphonic sounds of organizational truths. *Organization Studies* **29**(4): 525–541.

Szulanski, G. (1996). Exploring internal stickiness: Impediments to the transfer of best practice within the firm. *Strategic Management Journal* **17**(S2): 27–43.

Szulanski, G., R. Cappetta and R. J. Jensen (2004). When and how trustworthiness matters: Knowledge transfer and the moderating effect of causal ambiguity. *Organization Science* **15**(5): 600–613.

Szulanski, G., D. Ringov and R. J. Jensen (2016). Overcoming stickiness: How the timing of knowledge transfer methods affects transfer difficulty. *Organization Science* **27**(2): 304–322.

Townsend, D. M., R. A. Hunt, J. S. McMullen and S. D. Sarasvathy (2018). Uncertainty, knowledge problems, and entrepreneurial action. *Academy of Management Annals* **12**(2): 659–687.

Turcotte, W. E. (1974). Control systems, performance, and satisfaction in two state agencies. *Administrative Science Quarterly* **19**: 60–73.

Tushman, M. L. and D. A. Nadler (1978). Information processing as an integrating concept in organizational design. *Academy of Management Review* **3**(3): 613–624.

Tushman, M. L. and C. A. O'Reilly III (1996). Ambidextrous organizations: Managing evolutionary and revolutionary change. *California Management Review* **38**(4): 8–29.

Tversky, A. and D. Kahneman (1974). Judgment under uncertainty: Heuristics and biases. *Science* **185**(4157): 1124–1131.

Ulmer, R. R. and T. L. Sellnow (1997). Strategic ambiguity and the ethic of significant choice in the tobacco industry's crisis communication. *Communication Studies* **48**(3): 215–233.

Ulmer, R. R. and T. L. Sellnow (2000). Consistent questions of ambiguity in organizational crisis communication: Jack in the Box as a case study. *Journal of Business Ethics* **25**(2): 143–155.

Vakkuri, J. (2010). Struggling with ambiguity: Public managers as users of NPM-oriented management instruments. *Public Administration* **88**(4): 999–1024.

Van Dyne, L., S. Ang and I. C. Botero (2003). Conceptualizing employee silence and employee voice as multidimensional constructs. *Journal of Management Studies* **40**(6): 1359–1392.

Van Leeuwen, T. (2005). *Introducing social semiotics*. London, Routledge.

Vermeulen, F. (2018). A basic theory of inheritance: How bad practice prevails. *Strategic Management Journal* **39**(6): 1603–1629.

Walder, A. G. (2006). Ambiguity and choice in political movements: The origins of Beijing Red Guard factionalism. *American Journal of Sociology* **112**(3): 710–750.

Wang, P. and M. Jensen (2019). A bridge too far: Divestiture as a strategic reaction to status inconsistency. *Management Science* **65**(2): 859–878.

Ware, B. L. and W. A. Linkugel (1973). They spoke in defense of themselves: On the generic criticism of apologia. *Quarterly Journal of Speech* **59**(3): 273–283.

Weick, K. E. (1979). *The social psychology of organizing*. New York, McGraw-Hill.

Weick, K. (1983). Organizational communication: Toward a research agenda. In L. L. Putnam and M. E. Pacanowsky (Eds.), *Communication and organizations: An interpretive approach* (pp. 13–29). Newbury Park, Sage.

Weick, K. E. (1984). Small wins: Redefining the scale of social problems. *American psychologist* **39**(1): 40.

Weick, K. E. (1993). The collapse of sensemaking in organizations: The Mann Gulch disaster. *Administrative Science Quarterly* **38**(4): 628–652.

Weick, K. E. (1995). *Sensemaking in organizations*. Sage.

Weick, K. E. and K. M. Sutcliffe (2001). *Managing the unexpected*. San Francisco, Jossey-Bass.

Weick, K. E., K. M. Sutcliffe and D. Obstfeld (2005). Organizing and the process of sensemaking. *Organization Science* **16**(4): 409–421.

Wexler, M. N. (2009). Strategic ambiguity in emergent coalitions: The triple bottom line. *Corporate Communications: An International Journal* **14**(1): 62.

Williamson, O. E. (1979). Transaction-cost economics: The governance of contractual relations. *The Journal of Law and Economics* **22**(2): 233–261.

Wolbers, J., K. Boersma and P. Groenewegen (2018). Introducing a fragmentation perspective on coordination in crisis management. *Organization Studies* **39**(11): 1521–1546.

Wu, X. and F. Zhang (2014). Home or overseas? An analysis of sourcing strategies under competition. *Management Science* **60**(5): 1223–1240.

Zack, M. H. (2000). Managing organizational ignorance. In J. Woods and J. Cortada (Eds.), *The knowledge management yearbook 2000–2001* (pp. 353–373). Boston, Routledge.

Zuckerman, E. W. (1999). The categorical imperative: Securities analysts and the illegitimacy discount. *American Journal of Sociology* **104**(5): 1398–1438.

Zuckerman, E. W. (2000). Focusing the corporate product: Securities analysts and de-diversification. *Administrative Science Quarterly* **45**(3): 591–619.

Zuzul, T. W. (2019). "Matter Battles": Cognitive representations, boundary objects, and the failure of collaboration in two smart cities. *Academy of Management Journal* **62**(3): 739–764.

Acknowledgements

We gratefully thank the Series editors Nelson Phillips and Royston Greenwood, and the anonymous referees for their insightful comments and guidance. We also thank Giuseppe Delmestri, Renate Meyer, Evelyn Micelotta, Woody Powell, Robert Gibbons and the fellows of the Stanford CASBS Summer Institute on Organizations and their Effectiveness, as well as session attendants during presentations at research seminars at WU Wien and Bocconi University for their valuable suggestions. We are grateful to Umberto Platini and Meri Miettinen for the research assistance.

Organization Theory

Nelson Phillips
UC Santa Barbara

Nelson Phillips is Professor of Technology Management at UC Santa Barbara. His research interests include organization theory, technology strategy, innovation, and entrepreneurship, often studied from an institutional theory perspective.

Royston Greenwood
University of Alberta

Royston Greenwood is the Telus Professor of Strategic Management at the University of Alberta, a visiting professor at the University of Cambridge, and a visiting professor at the University of Edinburgh. His research interests include organizational change and professional misconduct.

Advisory Board
Paul Adler *USC*
Mats Alvesson *Lund University*
Steve Barley *University of Santa Barbara*
Jean Bartunek *Boston College*
Paul Hirsch *Northwestern University Ann Langley HEC Montreal Renate Meyer WU Vienna Danny Miller*
HEC *Montreal*
Mike Tushman *Harvard University*
Andrew Van de Ven *University of Minnesota*

About the Series
Organization theory covers many different approaches to understanding organizations. Its focus is on what constitutes the how and why of organizations and organizing, bringing understanding of organizations in a holistic way. The purpose of Elements in Organization Theory *is to systematize and contribute to our understanding of organizations.*

Cambridge Elements $\equiv$

Organization Theory

Printed in the United States
by Baker & Taylor Publisher Services